THE REVOLUTION
WILL BE HILARIOUS

THE REVOLUTION WILL BE HILARIOUS

ADAM MICHAEL KRAUSE

& OTHER ESSAYS

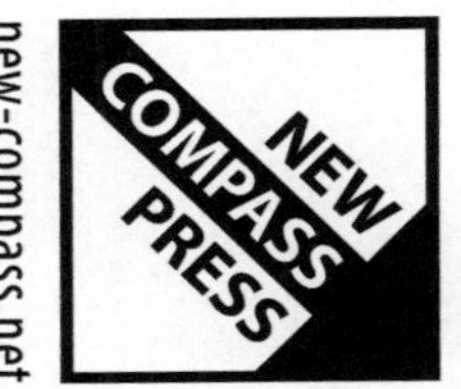

new-compass.net

The Revolution Will Be Hilarious
2018 © by Adam Krause

ISBN 978-82-93064-41-1
ISBN 978-82-93064-25-1 (ebook)

Published by New Compass Press
Grenmarsvegen 12
N–3912 Porsgrunn
Norway

Design and layout by Eirik Eiglad

New Compass presents ideas on participatory democracy, social ecology, and movement building—for a free, secular, and ecological society.

new-compass.net
2018

CONTENTS

INTRODUCTION

This collection of essays came about when New Compass Press informed me that the tiny pamphlet I had written for them, "The Revolution Will Be Hilarious," had proven just too tiny to publish economically. Rather than take it out of print, they asked, would I add some essays and let them do *The Revolution Will Be Hilarious and Other Essays*? My first thought was that this would be impossible. The things I had written since "The Revolution Will Be Hilarious" appeared in 2013 were very different in tone and style, and could seemingly never inhabit the same volume as that earlier essay.

"The Revolution Will Be Hilarious" uses the structure of jokes as an extended metaphor to explain the psychology of democracy. The essays I wrote after publishing it focus much more on the environmental apocalypse we are now experiencing. My tone became more urgent and strident—to such an extent that I even began using terms like "environmental apocalypse." "The Revolution Will Be Hilarious" seemed like a work from a simpler time, back when I thought we had more time.

Why the change in focus? The mistake I made, if it is a mistake, was adopting the habit of reading scientific journals. And recently, there has been a remarkable shift in tone. Rather than just saying that we have to do something or our environment will collapse, most scientists now seem to say that we have to do something because our environment is already collapsing. It is a subtle, but terrifying, shift. And there is no shortage of evidence to support it. Ice sheets are collapsing. Species are disappearing. Lakes are evaporating, making agriculture impossible in many places. People starve. The oceans are losing fish, but are filling with plastic. Things are not looking good. We are in the midst of something awful and unprecedented. Analyzing jokes to explain how democracy works suddenly seemed like an antiquated concern from a forgotten era.

But as I worked on some newer essays, under the impression that *The Revolution Will Be Hilarious and Other Essays* would be impossible, those seemingly quaint concerns came rushing back as central ones. In fact, some of the essays I assumed had supplanted "The Revolution Will Be Hilarious" actually precede and prepare the way for it.

The first piece in this volume, "THE END IS NEAR," was originally released on my own imprint, Red Earth Press. Each copy was hand-made, and there really weren't that many, so I am very excited for it to appear here, where at least the words can live on even after that limited edition disappears. "THE END IS NEAR" begins by discussing some of the many prophecies of apocalypse humans have heard in the preceding centuries. And since the world has been declared nearly over so often, why should we believe contemporary warnings of an environmental apocalypse? Well, as I mentioned above, because there is ample evidence that irreversible ecological collapse has already begun.

So if that's the case, how should we react? Do we panic? Stockpile gold? Build an army? Pray? Mostly, we need to get to work, but we don't need to panic, provided we get to work. And there are examples among those past prophets of doom who saw an impending apocalypse as a chance for transformation, not just fighting in the streets for the remaining crumbs.

In "THE END IS NEAR," I quote Naomi Klein's statement that "Mass uprisings of people—along the lines of the abolition movement and the Civil Rights Movement—represent the likeliest source of 'friction' to slow down an economic machine that is careening out of control."[1] I agree of course. But this statement requires elaboration. Both the abolition movement and the Civil Rights Movement were full of very contentious debates about tactics. If the time has already passed when we should have started a mass movement, the time has also passed when we should know how to proceed. Who are the targets? How do we stop them?

And although these are not topics we typically discuss aloud, is sabotage acceptable? What about violence?

So in "What Is To Be Done?, I analyze issues of ethics and tactics in political actions, with a special focus on the environmental movement. I did not begin writing this essay with a thesis to explain, but rather, a topic to explore. I had no idea what I would conclude, only that I would write. As such, this second essay took on a very different form from "THE END IS NEAR." In "THE END IS NEAR," I present short, often impressionistic explorations of various topics, and let the whole piece collectively present an idea. Sections are short. Topics shift. In "What Is To Be Done?" I explore the topic as I go, and the reader can follow my thoughts as I unpack a difficult subject and try to figure out how I really feel about it.

Although I began without a destination in mind, I eventually arrived somewhere, and much to my surprise, it was the idea that the revolution would be hilarious. In "What Is To Be Done?" I conclude that whatever movements we build or tactics we choose, those movements need to be inclusive and broad. So the lessons comedy can teach us about democracy are essential to answering the question of just what is to be done.

And so "The Revolution Will Be Hilarious" not only remains, but has proven itself essential. But for this new context, it was necessary to revise and expand the original text. I have no problem with that. Walt Whitman, who I refer to as the "patron saint" of "The Revolution Will Be Hilarious," first published *Leaves of Grass* in 1855, and then spent the rest of his life expanding and altering it in numerous editions of various lengths. So rewriting and revising previously published works is a practice with an impressive pedigree. Plus, an essay that spends so much time urging us to rethink our ideas and assumptions deserves to be periodically rethought.

In the time since its initial publication, various people have talked or written to me about "The Revolution Will Be Hilarious." In particular, Molly Shanahan utilized it while working on her doctoral thesis and sent me a number of helpful suggestions and observations. In particular, she suggested that "bisociation," a term I borrowed from Arthur Koestler, would make much more sense as "multisociation."

Following "The Revolution Will Be Hilarious" is "Buy The Land and Buy The Light," an essay originally presented as a paper at the Ecological Challenges Conference at the University of Oslo in 2017. Using businesses that sell the naming rights to stars as a starting point, I discuss changes in land ownership and usage in the capitalist era, with a particular focus on the United States. The notion that one can purchase a piece of property, put up a fence and then tear the earth to bits to extract resources (and no one can stop you because it's yours) is a very new and very dangerous idea that has somehow become accepted as common sense. The mistreatment of the original inhabitants of North America accelerated along with the development of these new notions of private property, and continue into the present, with battles over pipelines and fracked oil as an especially egregious example.

"The Revolution Will Be Hilarious" dances around various topics I couldn't actually discuss without making it an unreadable mess. "Time Is Not Money," acts almost as an appendix to "The Revolution Will Be Hilarious," clarifying some of the underlying ideas that essay leaves unsaid. And although it was composed from sections I cut from "The Revolution Will Be Hilarious," it ended up as a surprisingly cohesive piece on its own.

Concluding this volume is "Walking Each Other Home," another essay I published as a pamphlet on Red Earth Press. I wrote it after revisiting "The Revolution Will Be Hilarious" and it shows. I guess my writing has changed again. In "Walking Each Other Home," I explore the idea of "home." What is it? Why is it important? What does it mean to be homeless? How can anyone be "illegal"? The demands for openness, acceptance, and universal love made in "The Revolution Will Be Hilarious" are made again, but perhaps even more strongly and explicitly.

So this collection of essays begins with some rather urgent, occasionally depressing essays about the state of our planet, moves to a revised version of an older essay with comparatively more hope and positivity, and concludes with what I created after editing all that together. Life on Earth remains in incredible danger. I remain alarmed and angry. But in addition to that continuing rage, I have returned to emphasizing the seemingly simple notion that we must grow as a species, and learn to live in harmony with the natural world and one another. If we fail to do this, the end remains near. But I have returned to stating why and how we can change. And if I end up spending the rest of my life demanding that we treat each other and our shared habitat with love and respect, then I will, but hopefully humanity will wake up to the immense peril we are in very soon.

This seemed like an impossible project. I was ready to reject it. But by bringing it into existence, my writing and focus changed again. Carefully revising an older essay—an essay I thought I had moved beyond—caused various iterations of my writing self to collide and create a new one.

I am very proud of what appears in this book, but I could not have done it alone. A debt of gratitude goes to Eirik Eiglad and everyone else at New Compass Press for continuing to believe in me and my work. Endless thanks go to Marielle Allschwang for allowing me to read almost everything I write aloud to her, giving me more suggestions than I would ever care to count, agreeing to spend her life with me, and bringing me to that Shaker museum. I would also like to thank David Ravel and Richard Newman for taking me to meet Dabls. That was amazing.

It was a winding journey of exploration, research, and wildly different drafts that brought me to completing this volume. Creating it changed my thinking. Hopefully reading it can have a similar effect. I hope you enjoy it.

Time for the End of Time Again

> *— And as things fell apart,*
> *nobody paid much attention.*
>
> TALKING HEADS[2]

The end of the world has seemingly been upon us for as long as there has been a world, which makes it easy to dismiss and deride prophets of doom. A few thousand years ago, Jesus told his disciples that soon "the sun shall be darkened, and the moon shall not give her light, and the stars of heaven shall fall, and the powers that are in heaven shall be shaken."[3] And when would this occur? "Verily I say unto you, that this generation shall not pass, till all these things be done."[4] Standing before him was the last generation. The end of time was near.

And his followers believed it. The Epistle to the Hebrews, written around 63 or 64 CE, begins, "God, who at sundry times and in divers manners spake in times past unto the fathers by the prophets, hath in these last days spoken unto us by his son."[5] The First Epistle of John, written about thirty years later, states, "Little children, it is the last time: and as ye have heard that antichrist shall come, even now there are many antichrists; whereby we know that it is the last time."[6] Yet the world did not end.

Maybe Christ had been delayed. In 1806, in a village near Leeds, England, a hen laid an egg inscribed with the words "Christ Is Coming." Prayers were said. Skies were watched. There was repentance and panic. But the egg was either a forgery or the hen had been misinformed. Once again, the world did not end.[7]

In 1996, Sheldan Nidle, who claims to have been receiving extraterrestrial communications since he was a child, announced that 16 million spaceships, which is quite a few if you think about it, would arrive on December 17, heralding humanity's end. But the aliens did not arrive, and humanity carried on.[8]

More recently, a set of cycles in the Mayan's now-rarely-used calendar were set to cease in 2012, which some people decided meant the world would also end. But temporal units are human inventions, not facts of nature, so why one culture's means of marking time would impact the physical world is unclear. But a lot of people took this seriously. Once again, the world did not end.

These are just a few examples. An even remotely exhaustive list of apocalyptic predictions would fill volumes. There are always people who hope or fear they will be the last. Mostly hope. After all, it can be hard to pass the Earth on to the next generation and accept death and irrelevance. How much better it would be to stand at the end of history as the final generation—with gods, angels, or extraterrestrials on their way to let us know that there shall (of course) be none after us. But these portents of doom never show, and the world moves on. We are buried and forgotten.

The end of humanity is being predicted again. But this time, we probably shouldn't scoff. The reasons are more scientific, less supernatural, and for once, pretty convincing. We are destroying—or perhaps have already destroyed—the environment that sustains us. We are not near the end of humanity because gods or aliens have deemed us special, but because we're the idiots who couldn't figure out how to maintain our own habitat. And that shouldn't fuel anyone's hubris.

Here is a tiny sample of the current crop of prophets of doom. Linguist and political theorist Noam Chomsky writes that due to our terrifying combination of environmental destruction and rampant militarism, human civilization "may now be approaching its inglorious end."[9] The film director Werner Herzog stated in an interview, "I'm convinced that our presence on this planet is not sustainable, so we will be extinct fairly soon."[10] Journalist and environmentalist Bill McKibben writes, "We remain in denial about the peril that human civilization is in."[11] In his encyclical on the environment, Pope Francis writes, "Doomsday predictions can no longer be met with irony or disdain. We may well be leaving to coming generations debris, desolation, and filth."[12]

You Must Go On, I Can't Go On, I'll Go On

> *— Seems there's always more duty.*
> *Maybe that's the beauty.*

> MIKE WATT[13]

Rather than emanating from Pat Robertson or castrated cult members committing mass suicide in matching shoes, these recent apocalyptic predictions are different. Arctic ice is melting at increasing rates, giving us easier access to once-inaccessible fossil fuels. The irony of this would be hilarious if it weren't terrifying. Ice shelves in the Antarctic that were not expected to collapse for decades are already collapsing. Heatwaves, droughts, and wildfires are occurring with alarming frequency. And there are already more fossil fuels ready for use—claimed and accounted for by oil companies—than we can safely burn without experiencing total cataclysm. This is not narcissism. Humanity is approaching its end.

In an article about despair among climate scientists—people whose job it is to discover and explain all the bad news about our planet—Camille Parmesan of the University of Texas states:

To be honest, I panicked fifteen years ago—that was when the first studies came out showing that Arctic tundras were shifting from being a net sink to being a net source of CO2. That along with the fact this butterfly I was studying shifted its entire range across half a continent—I said this is big, this is big. Everything since then has just confirmed it.[14]

She continues, "Do I think it likely that the nations of the world will take sufficient action to stabilize climate in the next fifty years? No, I don't think it likely."[15] Which would of course be a rather problematic bit of inaction. As John H. Richardson states earlier in the article:

Arctic air temperatures are increasing at twice the rate of the rest of the world—a study by the U. S. Navy says that the Arctic could lose its summer sea ice by next year, eighty-four years ahead of the models—and evidence little more than a year old suggests the West Antarctic Ice Sheet is doomed, which will add between twenty and twenty-five feet to ocean levels. The one hundred million people in Bangladesh will need another place to live and coastal cities globally will be forced to relocate, a task complicated by economic crisis and famine—with continental interiors drying out, the chief scientist at the U. S. State Department in 2009 predicted a billion people will suffer famine within twenty or thirty years.[16]

What can we do to stop the destruction? The fossil fuel industry has an immense amount of power and money, and would love nothing more than to continue wielding power and amassing money. Politicians are bought. Disinformation campaigns are funded. What can we, with so much less power and money, do to stop them? After all, global capitalism is designed to generate the most profit for the fewest people in the shortest time. The Earth and most of its inhabitants are merely means to these ends. Resources are plundered indiscriminately, and the people living on top of those resources usually have too little power to stop the plunder. Landscapes become moonscapes. The rich get richer and the poor suffer. The rest of us remain largely indifferent for no reason whatsoever.

And we have prepared ourselves in the worst possible way to handle our coming catastrophes humanely. We just lived through the bloodiest and most genocidal century in history. As a point of comparison, somewhere between 3,000 and 5,000 people died in the Spanish Inquisition. That was pretty bad, but in the twentieth century, Stalin alone was responsible for ordering tens of millions of deaths. And that was just one bit of genocide in a century of genocide after genocide. Something has gone horribly wrong with humanity. We are not ready to handle our impending ecological disasters in ways that won't involve massive bloodshed, suffering, and despair. And the weapons we have now could kill every living thing on Earth. If that's really where we've gotten ourselves, our situation seems hopeless. So what can we do?

The interview in which Werner Herzog stated that "we will be extinct fairly soon" ends with the following exchange:

Q: Does our impending extinction worry you?

A: It doesn't make me nervous that we'll become extinct, it doesn't frighten me at all. There is a wonderful thing that Martin Luther the reformer said when he was asked, "What would you do if the world would disappear tomorrow in the apocalypse?" And Luther said, "Today, I would plant an apple tree."

Q: Do you believe in a superior being?

A: Oh, don't ask that—but if I knew that tomorrow a meteorite would destroy our planet, I would start shooting a new film today.[17]

Like Luther planting a tree whose fruit he knows he will never see, we ought to start that film, stop the fossil fuel industry from existing, end factory farming, ban nuclear weapons and nuclear power—so we don't kill ourselves by other means before we get the chance to save ourselves—and destroy militarism, nationalism, and borders. In spite of our apparently hopeless situation, we should not lose hope or stop trying.

Intense action now is our only hope. As individuals and as a species, we ought to follow the advice Miguel de Unamuno draws from Don Quixote: "Redress whatever wrong comes your way. Do now what must be done now and do here what must be done here."[18] As Naomi Klein writes, "Mass uprisings of people—along the lines of the abolition movement and the Civil Rights Movement—represent the likeliest source of 'friction' to slow down an economic machine that is careening out of control."[19]

The End Was Here

> *— Yeah it's all coming back to me now,*
> *my apocalypse, my apocalypse.*

BILL CALLAHAN[20]

Our economy and our world are not only careening out of control, but veering in the path of apocalypse. Or perhaps we've already smashed into it. Several years ago, I was riding in a van to a city I had never been. I was engrossed in a book. I looked up. We had entered the city. I was in one of many vehicles on the highway. The overpasses and underpasses were filled with cars reflecting the sun. It was a beautiful day. I felt perhaps the same exhilaration of movement and machines as Marinetti. It was the Kantian sublime, triggered by cars and concrete. I was overwhelmed with beauty and horror. Then it hit me. The world had already ended. We had poisoned the Earth. There was no hope. Our planet lay on its deathbed, drifting into oblivion, and we were driving on it. The apocalypse had passed with little notice, and we had entered the long, hard dénouement of human civilization. It was a strong, strange feeling, and it stuck with me.

In Alan Moore's comic book *Promethea*, there is an apocalypse. The story and the world, though transformed, continue. As one character says, "We all woke up, the day after the world ended, and we still had to feed ourselves and keep a roof over our heads. Life goes on, y'know? Life goes on."[21] The idea that an apocalypse is not necessarily an end makes etymological sense. "Apocalypse" comes from the

Greek for an uncovering or revelation. It is less destruction than disclosure. So maybe I was right. Maybe we've passed the apocalypse. But maybe life goes on after the world ends. And maybe there's still hope.

If we continue on our current path, we will doom billions of future humans to famines and wars. To quote Pope Francis again:

> The natural environment is a collective good, the patrimony of all humanity and the responsibility of everyone. If we make something our own, it is only to administer it for the good of all. If we do not, we burden our consciences with the weight of having denied the existence of others. That is why the New Zealand bishops asked what the commandment "Thou shall not kill" means when "twenty percent of the world's population consumes resources at a rate that robs the poor nations and future generations of what they need to survive."[22]

Our environmental crisis is also an ethical crisis. Our lifestyles are based on the exploitation and destruction of the natural world and the world's poor. The people of the first world denude and degrade the land on which far less politically powerful people live. All that death and destruction usually takes place far from us, so we don't have to watch. And we don't. But if we want to do anything even remotely close to the right thing, we will stop living as we do. The notion that our lifestyles won't need to change that much to save the Earth is nonsense. We don't just need to use better lightbulbs or something. Our lifestyles need to change. We cannot continue taking part in the murder of the Earth and its inhabitants.

Endgame Strategies

> *— It's after the end of the world!*
> *Don't you know that yet?*

> Sun Ra[23]

This is humanity's endgame. In chess, endgames occur when very few pieces remain on the board. Exactly when the middlegame ends and the endgame begins is often unclear, but endgames are distinct. Pawns become more important. Kings enter the open and attack. Poor endgame tactics can destroy a once-overwhelming advantage, while a cleverly waged endgame can turn a hopeless situation into a victory. Of course, not all games even get that far.

In Samuel Beckett's 1957 play *Endgame*, there is one act in one room. Hamm sits dying in his chair, unable to stand. Clov, limping and unable to sit, waits on him. There are also two trash cans on stage where Nell and Nagg live. There is a window stage left, and another stage right, but there is no light or life outside.

Hamm: Nature has forgotten us.

Clov: There's no more nature.

Hamm: No more nature! You exaggerate.

Clov: In the vicinity.

Hamm: But we breathe, we change! We lose our hair, our teeth! Our bloom! Our ideals!

Clov: Then she hasn't forgotten us.[24]

Nature only remains as rot, decay, and death. The other end of the life cycle has ceased. Nothing is born. Nothing is new.

Hamm: Did your seeds come up?

Clov: No.

Hamm: Did you scratch round them to see if they had sprouted?

Clov: They haven't sprouted.

Hamm: Perhaps it's too early.

Clov: If they were going to sprout they would have sprouted. (*Violently.*) They'll never sprout![25]

Throughout the play, the characters remain stuck in patterns. Hamm asks for his painkillers. Nell and Nagg reminisce. Clov walks from window to window, moving like a chess piece, limited by the rules of play and positions of pieces.

But there is a glimmer of hope near the end of the play. With Nagg and Nell dead, and Hamm about to die, Clov either sees or hallucinates a small boy outside in the distance. Hamm is unmoved. "If he exists he'll die there or he'll come here. And if he doesn't..."[26] Clov gets dressed and packed. He's leaving. But he might stay. The curtain closes. We don't know if he ever moves.

People rarely change until circumstances force them. And even then, people rarely change. Will we ever even try to save our habitat, or will we wait until there is no light, life, or love left, and then just stand there, still not quite sure if we should do something or not?

Do something.

Do something.

Do something.

Shaking Toward the Millennium

> *Hark! What means this dreadful sound?*
> *Hear the rumor all around!*
> *Wars and tumults greet our ears;*
> *Lo! The latter day appears.*
>
> SHAKER HYMN

We certainly need to do something, do something, do something, but what should we do? Action and hope, not fear and worry, are the answers. Christianity, a belief system obsessed with the end of the world, has dominated and shaped Western culture for thousands of years. We can learn a lot from the ways humans have reacted to all those regularly promised apocalypses. Terror and panic have not been the only reactions. Repentance and radical transformations have also occurred.

The Shakers, a millennial Christian group formed in the late 1700s, are of particular interest. Millennial movements are focused on the end of the world, with the idea of the millennium coming from the Book of Revelation, where it states:

> And I saw an angel come down from heaven, having the key of the bottomless pit and a great chain in his hand. And he laid hold on the dragon, that old serpent, which is the devil, and Satan, and bound him a thousand years. [...] And I saw thrones, and they sat upon them: and I saw the souls of them that were beheaded for the witness of Jesus, and for the word of God, and which had not worshipped the beast, neither his image, neither had received his mark upon their foreheads, or in their hands; and they lived and reigned with Christ a thousand years.[27]

Millennial movements believe the just will rule with Jesus for a thousand years, and there will be peace, prosperity, and plenty. Then the Devil will be released, and the final judgement will take place.

In the still nascent United States of the eighteenth century, the millennium was frequently declared imminent or already underway. In the 1740s, Jonathan Edwards sparked the Great Awakening, a millennial movement fueled by fears of hell fire. But the world never ended, and enthusiasm waned. Then in the 1770s, the New Light Stir revived millennial beliefs. Concurrent with the American Revolution, political upheaval added credence to the coming of a spiritual revolution. The Revolutionary War happened, but the devil was never chained, and Christ never came.

Or perhaps he did. And maybe he was a she. In 1747, John and Jane Wardley of Manchester, England broke from the Quakers and founded the Shakers in an attempt to recover the excitement and ecstatic millenarianism of the Quakers' early years.[28] A woman named Ann Lee joined them in 1758. She was soon declared the female manifestation of Christ, a unity of gender manifestations that completed the appearance of Christ on Earth, and thus heralded the millennium. In 1774, Ann Lee and a small band of Shakers left Manchester for a United States on the brink of rebellion.[29]

The Shakers were a millennial movement, but they had a peculiar notion of the second coming of Christ. For the Shakers, the millennium would be built by creating a critical mass of manifested Christs. The messiah would be a collective creation. Ann Lee's transformation was not only possible for everyone, but *required* of everyone. She was just the first to make the metamorphosis.

Ann Lee presented herself as a first among equals, not a special human fit for worship. "She refused to be deified. If her followers kneeled to her, she would kneel with them, saying, 'It is not me you love, but it is God in me.'"[30] She simply pointed the way toward perfection for everyone. And like their "Mother Ann," Shakers renounced family and sexual intercourse, so Christ could be manifested in humanity and the millennium could get underway. There would be peace, prosperity, and plenty.

In our present situation, the onset of the millennium is less a concern than the disappearance of the natural world. But whether we're Shakers in the eighteenth century or environmentally endangered beings in the twenty-first, a critical mass of changed minds is necessary. Radically new ways of seeing and being—total metamorphoses that overturn everything, manifested in everyone—are our only hope.

There is another lesson we can learn from the Shakers. They are remembered today, not for the end-time religion of Ann Lee, but for building Utopian communities and thoughtfully constructed furniture. Just as Jesus predicted an imminent end that never came, causing his followers to eventually give in and create structured organizations that could survive centuries, the Shakers made some of the longest lasting Utopian communities in modern history, an achievement "Ann Lee knew nothing of, and in which she would have taken no interest."[31]

Changed minds can be powerful and transformative. But changed minds that work together can reshape the world. To quote an essay entitled "'What Must I Do?' at the End of the World,"

> Faced with the catastrophe, there are those who get indignant, those who take note, those who denounce, and those who get organized. History depends on those who get organized.[32]

If our stories will be written in anything other than the fossil record, we can't just individually manifest new modes of thinking. We'll need to harmoniously orchestrate our actions—not as a single, rigid being, but as a beautiful array of illuminated minds, attacking our problems from every angle. Humans made this mess, and we can unmake it. Revolutions are required, but they'll differ from those of centuries past. Rather than dethroning kings from solitary seats of power so we can take their place, we need to dethrone everyone, then destroy the thrones, share our power, and work together.

The end is near. But it doesn't have to be.

WHAT IS TO BE DONE?

— I might be ready to embrace a snake, but, if one comes to bite you, I should kill it and protect you.

Mohandas Gandhi[33]

Roughly two years before the beginning of the U.S. Civil War, the abolitionist John Brown raided a federal armory in Virginia, in the hopes of provoking the violent destruction of slavery. His raid failed and he was hanged. A small segment of the Northern population saw him as a martyr. Most called him insane. Southerners almost unanimously declared him a terrorist. And Insane. *The Richmond Whig*, in a typical statement, declared that "the murderous old traitor and murderer belongs to the gallows, and the gallows will have its own."[34]

In the time between John Brown's arrest and execution, Henry David Thoreau delivered a lecture entitled "A Plea For Captain John Brown" in Concord, Massachusetts. Usually the town bell would ring when a lecture was about to begin, but Thoreau's topic was so controversial that no one was willing to ring it. So Thoreau rang it himself. Upon returning to the lectern, he said it was John Brown's "peculiar doctrine that a man has a perfect right to interfere by force with the slaveholder, in order to rescue the slave. I agree with him."[35]

John Brown was very violent. Praise for him may sound strange coming from the same Thoreau who helped inspire Mohandas Gandhi and Martin Luther King, Jr. to utilize nonviolent civil disobedience in their struggles—the same Thoreau of whom King writes, "During my student days I read Henry David Thoreau's 'On Civil Disobedience' for the first time. Here, in this courageous New Englander's refusal to pay his taxes and his choice of jail rather than support a war that would spread slavery's territory into Mexico, I made my first contact with the theory of nonviolent resistance."[36] And Gandhi states that "Thoreau was a great writer, philosopher, poet, and withal a most practical man, that is, he taught nothing he was not prepared to practice in himself. He was one of the greatest and most moral men America has produced."[37]

Rather than pay a tax to support an imperialist war to expand slave territory, Thoreau went to jail. He was only there one night, but the essay he wrote about it, "On Civil Disobedience," had a monumental impact. In it, he writes,

"Unjust laws exist: shall we be content to obey them, or shall we endeavor to amend them, and obey them until we have succeeded, or shall we transgress them at once?"[38] Like Thoreau refusing to pay his tax, King and Gandhi disobeyed bad laws. Both did so nonviolently. The one time we know Thoreau performed civil disobedience, it was nonviolent, yet in "A Plea For Captain John Brown," he writes, "I do not wish to kill or be killed, but I can foresee circumstances in which both these things would be by me unavoidable."[39]

King and Gandhi, and Gandhi in particular, took the nonviolent part of nonviolent resistance pretty seriously. Shortly before the Second World War, Gandhi wrote an open letter to Nazi Germany's Jewish citizens. "If there ever could be a justifiable war in the name of and for humanity, a war against Germany, to prevent the wanton persecution of a whole race, would be justified. But I do not believe in any war."[40] So what would he do instead? "If I were a Jew and were born in Germany and earned my livelihood there, I would claim Germany as my home even as the tallest gentile German may, and challenge him to shoot me or cast me in the dungeon."[41]

As Saul Alinsky writes in *Rules for Radicals*, "Gandhi's passive resistance would never have had a chance against a totalitarian state such as that of the Nazis. It is dubious whether under those circumstances the idea of passive resistance would even have occurred to Gandhi."[42] In totalitarian states, members of the opposition have a strange tendency to disappear in the middle of the night. Getting arrested or shot to call attention to injustice is not going to be a particularly effective tactic.

So Gandhi's advice seems pretty terrible. But does it seem terrible because we know from history just how ruthless Germany's genocidal war machine was? Or do we simply feel that violence is justified when someone seeks to destroy us? If someone tries to kill you, you probably feel warranted fighting back. And if I am standing nearby and can prevent your death, you probably won't mind if I use whatever level of violence proves necessary to save you. Similarly, if some government or group of people seeks to exterminate you and everyone else of your race or religion, violent self-defense seems reasonable. And if I had an army and could prevent your genocide, you might not mind if we did what armies do. So most of us are willing to accept violence in cases of legitimate self-defense.

Just What Is Self-Defense?

But once we accept violence for self-defense, things get quite complicated. When is something so threatening that violence becomes admissible? When are we fighting for our lives, and when are we just fighting? Most of history's truly heinous acts were performed in the name of self-defense. No one goes around thinking, "I'm an unjust aggressor." Rather, we assume we are on the side of right and good, and then rationalize our violent actions by expanding "self-defense" to cover whatever we have done or are about to do.

During the Russian Revolution of 1917, the Bolshevik Party found itself embroiled in a brutal civil war. Communism, which they aimed to create, would generate wealth rationally and distribute it equally. But poverty was becoming universal instead. They had promised peace, land, and bread, but this was proving difficult. They figured a new world could still result from the revolution, but if they failed, the future would be as bleak as the past. You see, they were defending humanity.

So Leon Trotsky, the People's Commissar of War, used the Bolshevik's Red Army to destroy rival parties and consolidate power. The Bolsheviks were the vanguard of the revolution, after all. To maintain discipline in his ranks, he executed his own retreating troops.[43] Then, as the civil war wound down, work became compulsory and "deserters from labor" were sent to concentration camps.[44] And in March 1921, sailors at Kronstadt, whom Trotsky had previously called "the pride and glory of the revolution," demanded the rights and freedoms the Bolsheviks had promised. So Trotsky took his troops and massacred the sailors.[45]

Of course, all that violence never produced a free and equal society, but one of history's most brutal and repressive regimes. That regime, the Soviet Union, not only survived the civil war, but spent much of the twentieth century spreading its system across the globe, largely through violence, and largely in the name of creating Utopia. But Utopia never arrived. Just more bloodshed and repression.

There were inevitable clashes and proxy wars between the Soviet Union and the United States, which was simultaneously spreading *its* system across the globe, also largely through violence, but in the name of bringing free-market capitalism to every nation on Earth. By obstructing Communist advances, they too were defending humanity. This also tended to create bloodshed and repression.

To take just one example, in September 1970, Salvador Allende of Chile became the first Marxist elected president anywhere in the Western Hemisphere. Pepsi-Cola and ITT, two U.S. corporations operating in Chile, mentioned to Richard Nixon that they were worried what an Allende presidency would mean for them. Ascendant socialism endangered capitalism. So Nixon and his Secretary of State Henry Kissinger used the CIA to orchestrate Allende's overthrow. On September 11, 1973, Augusto Pinochet, with the U.S. Government's funding and assistance, staged a military coup. Salvador Allende was shot in his office. But he was hardly the only person murdered. Two sports stadiums were turned into camps for interrogation, torture, and execution. And atrocities continued throughout the nearly two decades of Pinochet's rule. Thousands of Chileans were murdered by their own government. And all of this was set in motion to keep the free-market free by keeping a legally elected Marxist out of office. But communism is dangerous, and the market is good, so all that death was justified. You see, it was self-defense.

Since it is very easy to tell ourselves we are acting in self-defense when we are actually the aggressors, we need to be careful just what we call self-defense. Humans have successfully rationalized terrible acts in its name. Caution is required.

Defending Ourselves

And caution is required because the planet and its inhabitants are under attack, and we need to determine what we can do.

As Rebecca Solnit points out, climate change is inherently violent. Businesses and governments that "continue to profit off the rapid, violent, and intentional destruction of the Earth" are committing "extreme, horrific, longterm, widespread violence."[46] Or as Adrian Parr stated in an interview with the *New York Times*, "The human species is the agent of a terrible injustice being perpetrated against other species, future generations, ecosystems, and our fellow human beings."[47]

There are already crop failures and droughts, heat waves that kill thousands, undrinkable water, and acidified oceans where shellfish can no longer form shells. In India, heatstroke deaths have increased by 61% in the last decade.[48] The heat there can be so intense that just going outdoors can mean death.[49] And the subsequent drought is so extreme that suicides among farmers have risen dramatically.[50] And that's just India. In Africa, droughts and water shortages due to rapid changes in climate have already placed more than 31 million people at risk of death from starvation and malnutrition.[51] One person starving to death is a tragedy. 31 million is a tragedy of such magnitude that it's almost impossible to comprehend. We can no longer talk about a *looming* environmental crisis. The crisis has begun. The Earth and its inhabitants are under attack. But by whom? All of us? Some of us? If it's all of us, then maybe we should get together and stop doing what we're doing.

Of course, it's not that simple. There is not some undifferentiated and abstracted "humanity" destroying the world. It is those who profit most from the "rapid, violent, and intentional destruction of the Earth" who bear the most responsibility. The world's poor, whose lives and livelihoods these profiteers destroy, should not share equally in the blame. The poor should be defended. The profiteers should be stopped. We should not blame "humanity," but a specific segment of humans. So if the Earth is under violent attack by certain humans, can we feel justified if we fight back? This planet sustains us and we have nowhere else to go.

Just imagine if the source of all this destruction were a more obvious enemy. Imagine a malevolent alien race just landed, started removing and destroying our resources, killing the oceans, causing an unprecedented rate of species extinction, pouring pollutants into rivers, cutting the tops off mountains, and warming our atmosphere to dangerous levels. If that were the case, any human who didn't take up arms to defend our common home would be branded a coward. But because other humans perform precisely that same list of atrocities upon our planet, the path to stopping that destruction is much less clear. The strict lines of demarcation between "us" and "them" that would exist if those malevolent aliens had landed are hazy. So we can't just take up arms and start shooting. The enemy is everywhere. The enemy is not only within our societies, but often runs them. The army and police are employees of the polluters. So how do we proceed?

Singing Songs and Carrying Signs

It has proven rather difficult to stop environmental degradation by passing laws. For example, hydraulic fracturing, or fracking, involves pumping wastewater into subterranean rocks to release fossil fuels. Artificially induced earthquakes are among the many environmental dangers fracking produces. Natural and artificial earthquakes differ in several respects, allowing researchers to quantify the instance of each. Induced earthquakes occur at shallower average depths, causing greater ground-shaking, and more often occur in swarms. In Oklahoma, where fracking has been on the rise, an average of 1.5 earthquakes with a magnitude of 3.0 or greater occurred annually between 1950 and 2005. Between 2005 and 2015, a period that coincides with the introduction of increased fracking to the area, that number jumped to several hundred per year, "many of which are thought to be related to wastewater injection."[52]

Fracking is terribly dangerous and damaging to the Earth. So in November 2014, nearly 60% of Denton, Texas voted to ban fracking within city limits. Lawsuits against the decision were filed within hours, and state representative Drew Darby introduced House Bill 40, which is designed to take oil and gas extraction out of municipal hands. It declares that:

> A municipality or other political subdivision may not enact or enforce an ordinance or other measure, or an amendment or revision of an existing ordinance or other measure, that bans, limits, or otherwise regulates an oil and gas operation within its boundaries or extraterritorial jurisdiction.[53]

Under HB40, which was passed into law, the State of Texas, rather than the cities in question, can say what oil and gas companies may do. Furthermore, all decisions need to be "commercially reasonable"—"a condition that permits a reasonably prudent operator to fully, effectively, and economically exploit, develop, produce, process, and transport oil and gas."[54] Similarly, in May 2016, the Colorado State Supreme Court declared a series of municipal fracking bans invalid, while also using the court's written opinion to block any future efforts to ban fracking anywhere else in the state.[55] One of the decisions declares that any fracking ban is unacceptable, as it "materially impedes the effectuation of the state's interest in the efficient and responsible development of oil and gas resources."[56] These are all clear moves to take power away from those fracking harms the most while keeping it in the hands of those doing the harm and reaping the profits.

In a much more violent example, Berta Cáceres—a Honduran indigenous rights activist, environmentalist, and one of the main members of the opposition to the regime running Honduras at the time of her death—was murdered in her home in 2016. She had spent years fighting the construction of the Agua Zarca Dam, an environmentally destructive project that not only uses land belonging to the Lenca people, but jeopardizes their access to water. According to international law, they should have been consulted. But that never happened.

Many assume that Cáceres' death was a political execution. Her nephew stated that "Everyone is saying that the government or the company did it, but you'll never know. It's the art of obfuscation."[57] The government her nephew sees as a chief suspect arose from a 2009 coup that forcibly deposed President Manuel Zelaya. Almost every nation in the Organization of American Sates pushed for his return and for elections not run by the de facto coup regime. But U.S. Secretary of State Hillary Clinton helped prevent his return, in order to "render the question of Zelaya moot,"[58] a statement she makes in the hardcover edition of her book, *Hard Choices*, that was subsequently removed from the paperback, along with everything else pertaining to the Honduran coup. (An email sent by the U.S. Ambassador to Honduras in the immediate aftermath of the coup had informed Clinton that "there is no doubt that the military, Supreme Court and National Congress conspired on June 28 in what constituted an illegal and unconstitutional coup against the Executive Branch."[59] She later rewrote history in an attempt to defend her actions, stating that "the legislature in Honduras and the national judiciary actually followed the law in removing President Zeleya."[60]) Elections were held, but every organization monitoring them refused to stay. Every organization, that is, except the U.S. Republican Party. The coup regime, to no one's surprise, won. Violence and repression rose, and Berta Cáceres was eventually murdered in her home for opposing a dam being built illegally.

"Unjust laws exist: shall we be content to obey them, or shall we endeavor to amend them, and obey them until we have succeeded, or shall we transgress them at once?"[61] In all these cases, making and amending laws failed. You can fight for laws banning fracking, but those laws will be overturned. You can pass laws protecting indigenous people and their land, but those laws will be ignored. You can protest, but depending where you live, that might get you killed. And representatives of the most powerful government on Earth will lie and rewrite history, just to make sure that transnational capital can do whatever it pleases. Passing laws in defense of the Earth has either become impossible, or when possible, pointless.

So is nonviolent civil disobedience still a viable answer? Or has this, like laws protecting the environment, become something industrial capitalists and the politicians that support them have learned to accept and ignore? As Derrick Jensen writes in *Endgame*, there are many protests in which

> Protest organizers provide police with estimates of the numbers of people who have volunteered to be arrested (so police can schedule the right number of paddy wagons), and also provide police with potential arrestee's IDs so the process of arrest will be smooth and easy on everyone involved. It's a great system, guaranteed to make all parties feel good. The police feel good because they've kept the barbarians from the gates, the activists feel good because they've made a stand—*I got arrested for what I believe in*—and those in power feel good because nothing much has changed.[62]

And since nothing much has changed, the existing system remains in place, and the violence against the Earth and the world's poor continues. A game is played and nothing is accomplished.

Nonviolent civil disobedience certainly seems less effective now than it did during the Civil Rights Movement. In *Direct Action: An Ethnography*, David Graeber writes:

> Fifty years ago, during the Civil Rights Movement, there was a brief moment in American history where Gandhian

tactics worked: the violence lying behind racial segregation was laid bare across America in terrifying images of racist sheriffs with police dogs. Perhaps this was a very particular set of circumstances: for instance, the fact that so many northern reporters saw the South as an alien country anyway. Or perhaps in the intervening half-century something has changed about the American media. Whatever the reason, this feat has not been repeated; largely, it would seem, because those making the editorial decisions feel their ultimate loyalties are to the very larger structure of power Gandhian strategies mean to expose.[63]

Furthermore, as Nicholas Mirzoeff stated in an interview, "Today, if police dogs attack demonstrators, it is no longer national news. Ironically, the example of King himself, so often vilified as a traitor and a Communist in his lifetime, is used to berate today's protesters with the demand for nonviolence, meaning compliance with police instructions. King never intended nonviolence to mean compliance with the state."[64] The state determines who may occupy a public space and what they may do there. And the state has given itself the sole right to utilize force. Only the police can bring dogs or weapons to protests. When anyone else does, it's a downright abomination. Violence must always come from above. When it comes from below, our outrage is expected.

Just how we can make our actions effective is not obvious. As Daniel McGowan, who was convicted of terrorism for performing two arsons with the Earth Liberation Front, states in the documentary *If A Tree Falls: A Story of the Earth Liberation Front*:

> The situation with the environment is not getting better, it's getting worse. And I'm not saying the path of destruction or destroying everything is the right path. But I didn't know what to do. It's like when you're screaming at the top of your lungs and no one hears you, like, what the hell are you supposed to say?[65]

The planet that sustains us is in grave danger. But getting much of anyone to recognize this very simple and frightening fact is proving quite difficult. Laws are ignored. Protests are theatre. Sabotage and violence discredit.

Fighting Back

But one thing is certain. We can no longer wait patiently while nation-states spend decades debating non-binding environmental agreements that accomplish nothing. It is increasingly obvious that increasingly intense and disruptive actions are required. That's easy enough to say. But this seemingly simple statement raises some complex ethical issues. What is permissible in defense of the Earth? Elsewhere, I have quoted Naomi Klein's statement that "Mass uprisings of people—along the lines of the abolition movement and the Civil Rights Movement—represent the likeliest source of 'friction' to slow down an economic machine that is careening out of control."[66] She makes this claim and fails to elaborate. When I quoted it, I also failed to elaborate. But this statement *requires* elaboration. Within both the abolition movement and the Civil Rights Movement, the choice between violence and nonviolence was incredibly contentious. William Lloyd

Garrison and John Brown, Martin Luther King, Jr. and the Black Panthers, all adopted widely divergent tactics in pursuit of many of the same goals. If there is going to be a mass movement in defense of the Earth, and there absolutely needs to be, similar controversies will certainly arise. We cannot ignore them.

The arguments for getting belligerent are compelling. If the contemporary ruling classes are among the most destructive people in the history of the planet, and have deemed just about anything permissible in pursuit of their aims, why should we act in collusion with their police forces to act out almost entirely ineffectual forms of protest? Why should we push for legislation that will be ignored or repealed? How can we become actual agents of social change, rather than players of a rigged game?

In recent decades, more confrontational tactics for defending the environment were utilized by Earth First!, co-founded by Dave Foreman and three others in 1980. Foreman had worked for the Wilderness Society and the Nature Conservancy, but became disillusioned when he saw that such mainstream environmental organizations could only achieve token gestures and symbolic successes. As he wrote in 1982, "The Forest Service is Louisiana-Pacific's. Interior is Exxon's. The Environmental Protection Agency is Dow's."[67] Earth First! declared extralegal tactics necessary in defense of wilderness. One of their earliest newsletters states that "Lobbying, lawsuits, magazines, press releases, outings, and research papers are fine. But they are not enough. EARTH FIRST will use them, but we will also use demonstrations, confrontations, and more creative tactics and rhetoric."[68]

Those actions were, and are, largely nonviolent, although one of their slogans, "No compromise in defense of Mother Earth," seems to imply an acceptance of whatever proves necessary. They popularized tree-spiking, which involves hiding large nails, or "spikes," in trees. These spikes can destroy equipment and injure whoever hits one with a chainsaw. But lumber companies are usually informed once the spikes are in place, and the trees are usually spared. Although there have been injuries, it is most often only a potentially violent act. Beyond tree-spiking, there were other acts of sabotage and attempted sabotage. In 1989, Foreman and three others were arrested for intent to damage power lines leading to the Rock Flats nuclear weapons facility in Colorado.[69] Can we accept sabotage, especially when it obstructs the destruction of the planet that sustains us? Is that legitimate self-defense?

In a book about the dangers of suburban sprawl, Oliver Gillham writes about another group and another bit of sabotage.

One of the most extreme expressions of anti-sprawl sentiment occurred in December 2000, when the Earth Liberation Front (an ecoterrorist group) went so far as to set fire to several houses being built in a new subdivision in Suffolk County, New York. Spray painted messages on the houses read "Stop Urban Sprawl" and "If You Build It We Will Burn It." While no one on either side of the sprawl debate condones such violent action, the incident does demonstrate how inflammatory the subject has become.[70]

It seems mistaken to both make that "inflammatory" pun, and to say that "no one on either side of the sprawl debate condones such violent action." The ELF placed themselves so emphatically in the debate that someone writing a book on the subject would feel the need to mention them in the introduction. In fact, it seems important to ask: can we countenance the destruction of unsold and unfinished houses whose construction destroys our planet? Is that kind of arson legitimate self-defense? If developers' idea of "development" is destroying every remaining inch of the natural world, shouldn't we stop them? Is arson an acceptable answer?

In the over 1,200 actions attributed to the Earth Liberation Front and the Animal Liberation Front, no one has ever been killed or injured. Yet those who have been caught are often tried as terrorists. As Bill Barton of the Native Forest Council states in *If A Tree Falls*:

> The industry tends to call the environmentalists "radical." The reality is that 95% of the standing native forests in the United States have been cut down. It's not radical to try and save the last 5%. What's radical is logging 95%.[71]

The people behind oil spills and other environmental disasters get fines. The people who try to stop them get prison time. Something is very wrong with this.

In the early 1980s, about a decade before the formation of the ELF, a Canadian group called Direct Action bombed a power plant substation on Vancouver Island and a factory in Toronto where guidance systems for cruise missiles were produced. The power plant Direct Action bombed was being built in an area that didn't really need it. The whole project had been approved without community oversight, and it was rumored that the plant's real purpose was to sell excess energy to the United States, which ended up looking like the truth once it was up, running, and sending much of its power to California. Direct Action bombed the plant while it was still under construction—after the most expensive equipment was in place, but before it was providing power. This was meant to hurt the project financially, but not alienate the public with a blackout. No one was injured, and the project was delayed.

If no one was hurt, was this action violent? Is destruction justified if it aims to stop even greater destruction? Is violence just one thing, or are there many types, differentiated by target, intent, and severity? Or, to quote the Dalai Lama, perhaps "the distinction between violence and non-violence lies less in the nature of the action and more in the motivation with which it is done."[72]

Compared to that first action, the subsequent bombing of the weapons plant in Toronto went much less smoothly. Direct Action parked a van filled with explosives next to one of the buildings and called in a warning. But the timer went off early, the building had not been vacated, and although no one died, many were severely injured. Juliet Belmas, who made the phone call, later stated that "to this day I believe it was a miracle no one was killed, we should never have attacked a civilian target (a place where people worked) with 550 pounds of dynamite; it was wacko crazy."[73] Watching the aftermath on television, and seeing paramedics carrying people out on stretchers, Ann Hansen, another member of

Direct Action responsible for the bombing, writes that she felt "the inescapable guilt of having seriously injured innocent people."[74] She considered suicide.

In her memoirs, Hansen's main accomplice in the bombing, Brent Taylor, states, "If people are building weapons of destruction to maintain their wealth and power, I see nothing wrong with destroying those weapons."[75] So is obstructing the construction of weapons capable of destroying all life on Earth self-defense? Or had Direct Action, like Nixon and Trotsky, used the notion of self-defense to defend the indefensible? Maybe they had taken it too far? In an interview with *prisontv. net*, Taylor stated, "We always took it a little farther, sort of to a Unabomber level, really."[76]

Acting in Isolation

The Unabomber is the name the United States Federal Bureau of Investigation gave Ted Kaczynski as they sought to determine his identity and arrest him for killing three people and injuring 23 others with homemade bombs over the course of 17 years. Kaczynski was a mathematics prodigy, who was admitted to Harvard at 16 and earned his doctorate from the University of Michigan at 24. He taught at the University of California, Berkeley for two years, but abruptly resigned, moving to a cabin in Montana, where he hoped to live off the land. But "developers" were destroying the land. As he stated in an interview:

> The best place, to me, was the largest remnant of this plateau that dates from the tertiary age. It's kind of rolling country, not

> flat, and when you get to the edge of it you find these ravines that cut very steeply in to cliff-like drop-offs and there was even a waterfall there. It was about a two days hike from my cabin. That was the best spot until the summer of 1983. That summer there were too many people around my cabin so I decided I needed some peace. I went back to the plateau and when I got there I found they had put a road right through the middle of it. You just can't imagine how upset I was. It was from that point on I decided that, rather than trying to acquire further wilderness skills, I would work on getting back at the system. Revenge.[77]

He initially performed small acts of sabotage on those nearby developments, but soon started mailing bombs to university professors and airlines in a rather misguided attempt to destroy the entire system that had made so much destruction possible.

In 1995, Kaczynski promised to stop his bombings if a major newspaper or magazine would publish his manifesto, "Industrial Society and Its Future." *The New York Times* and *The Washington Post* both did. His brother recognized the prose and ideas, the FBI had its first real lead, and Kaczynski was soon arrested.

Although the preservation of wilderness was his main concern, his manifesto rarely addresses it. Writing in the first person plural, either to hide his numbers, or perhaps as a tacit admission that a lone murderer is easily dismissed as insane while groups are worth taking seriously, he writes, "Since there are well-developed environmental and wilderness movements, we have written very little about environmental degradation or the destruction of wild nature, even though we consider these to be highly important."[78] Instead, he lashes out at "leftism," "technology," "political correctness," and "oversocialization."

For Kaczynski, "oversocialization" involves total adaptation to the existing social order and its values. And although becoming a productive member of a society dedicated to demolishing the Earth is certainly something to avoid, Kaczynski's violent, antisocial response is not the right one. Humans are social creatures. We live, work, and develop together. Social transformations come from collective endeavors. The best way to replace our dominant paradigm is to create and inhabit institutions that actually embody freedom, justice, and environmentally harmonious modes of being. This requires movements, which require groups of people. Of course, these will often be small. Truly radical change is rarely popular at the outset. Abolitionists constituted a very small, marginalized group. Yet slavery was still evil. Real social change, maybe without exception, starts small. But as groups become smaller, amoral measures become more likely. Kaczynski acted alone. Direct Action had five members and acted in isolation. Cut off from wider social movements, ethical oversight can disappear. Small may be beautiful, but too small can be a real problem.

In *If A Tree Falls*, activist and filmmaker Tim Lewis discusses the collapse of the environmental movement in Eugene, Oregon in the wake of the ELF arsons:

> I think people were self-righteous, I think people thought they had the answer, weren't willing to listen to other points of view,

because their view was more radical than that point of view. All of that came into play, I think, to help narrow the amount of people that were connected within the movement to the point where it just went—poof—doesn't exist anymore.[79]

In addition, groups and individuals utilizing more violent methods cannot collaborate with those acting in open opposition. On simple, tactical grounds, legal and extralegal groups cannot know what one another are up to. Those who need secrecy will blow their cover, while those acting in the open will be discredited by association. Extralegal activity almost unavoidably entails isolation. And once stripped of the social, ethics can become irrelevant.

In a letter to *Earth First!*, Kaczynski writes, "Concerning EF!, my suggestion is that the real revolutionaries among them should withdraw from the existing EF! movement, which would exclude mere reformers, liberals, leftists, etc. who are afraid of 'alienating the middle class.'"[80] Given the histories of previous movements, this seems somewhat logical. Small bands of inspired minorities tend to have the greatest impact. But if the "real revolutionaries" take on everyone else, then everyone else becomes the enemy, and anything becomes possible.

Acting Together

Since none of us can dismantle our existing systems on our own, to change our social order, we must remain social. But this is not to say that larger groups, like nations or armies or mobs, have not marched off and committed any heinous acts. That's pretty much what "history" is. War after war after genocide. Large groups are not somehow more moral than individuals. The opposite is usually the case. But if we wish to mount any political resistance against the existing order, acting alone is almost always going to be a bad idea. But working together can go pretty poorly too.

In Stanley Milgram's controversial experiments at Yale University, two subjects, a "teacher" and a "learner," were led into a room. The "learner" was strapped to a chair, and an electrode was placed on one wrist. The "teacher" was told the experiment was meant to measure the effects of punishment on learning. Then the "teacher" quizzed the "learner" on a series of word pairs. Every time an error was made, the "teacher" administered an increasing level of shock.

Except the "learner" was an actor, the electrode was a prop, and the real object of the experiment was how much pain the average person would inflict just because a scientist at a prestigious university told them to.

> At 75 volts, the "learner" grunts. At 120 volts he complains verbally; at 150 he demands to be released from the experiment. His protests continue as the shocks escalate, growing increasingly vehement and emotional. At 285 volts, his response can only be described as an agonizing scream.[81]

At each point, the scientist urges the "teacher" to continue. The assumption that only a sadistic fringe would shock the "learner" at the most extreme level would make roughly two-thirds of humanity part of that sadistic fringe. Which is not exactly a "fringe." And since people are so easily led to bad behavior, the ways we act together, and what we demand of each other, are incredibly important.

What Is To Be Done?

There may be no universally appropriate tactics for undermining our existing systems. Time, place, context, and endless experimentation will determine what is to be done. In totalitarian states, volunteering to get arrested as a form of protest isn't actually protest, but suicide. So the more oppressive the state, the more likely it is that opposition to it will be a militia with guns and not a nonprofit with picket signs. But in a more open society, immediately adopting violent tactics can discredit entire movements.

Right now, it is necessary to stand in the way of those who would destroy the planet to maintain power and profit. Tactics will vary by location and political climate. But in every case, this needs to be both a *social* movement and an *ethical* movement. Actions enacted in anger and isolation, as well as actions enacted by larger groups, can all be problematic. No path is perfect. Means and methods will always shift. We should never get stuck in patterns or stop analyzing what we do, and should always be wary of the voice that urges us to continue with an act we may regret.

Whether we are prepared or not, we are entering a new epoch. Taking some sort of action will soon become unavoidable. Fossil fuels, which power global capitalism's destruction of the Earth, are going to disappear or become too expensive to extract profitably. By some accounts, we have already passed peak oil. Cars, trucks, airplanes, global shipping, plastics, and many other now-ubiquitous facts of life will become relics of an unrecoverable past. We can always return to the Stone Age, but the Oil Age is only going to happen once. And it's almost over. Without fossil fuels, industrial capitalism will become impossible. Will it be a sad ending for everyone but the insects, or a transition to a better future? The current status quo is already doomed. Their doom will be our demise if we don't hasten their downfall. But how do we do that? What is permissible?

We ought to recognize that humans are more easily moved to extreme actions than we are usually willing to admit. Robespierre didn't need to do all that much to produce his terror. A few impassioned speeches, and the lines for the guillotine stretched around the block. As our situation grows increasingly dire, just what methods we can adopt needs to be clear. If there is to be a mass movement that confronts and disrupts the entrenched powers destroying our planet, there will certainly be debates about tactics. We don't necessarily need definitive answers in place before we begin. After all, it's already past time to act. But we need to be ready to apply constant vigilance to those actions. We need to get organized. But we need to make intelligent and effective organizations. We have to get it right this time. It might be our last chance.

THE REVOLUTION WILL BE HILARIOUS

I can't understand why people are frightened of new ideas.
I'm frightened of the old ones.

JOHN CAGE[82]

The acts of thinking comedically and behaving democratically share enough analogous elements that an extended comparison between the two makes each much clearer. In particular, comedy can help elucidate the type of thinking it will take to create and maintain a free and democratic society, generate new ideas, and foster broad social movements.

The ideas presented here should be useful to anyone. My intended audience is not simply comedians or even fans of comedy. It is not even written for funny people. Just people. Wherever they might be.

As will be shown, comedy can teach us a great deal about the type of thinking it will take to create a better world. Just as jokes require understanding and utilizing concealed connections for comedic effect, free societies require comprehending, tolerating, and putting those same connections to use. A mind that only perceives one correct mode of being is both inherently undemocratic and invariably humorless. In order to make jokes or communicate effectively with people outside one's immediate circle, one must have knowledge of, and an ability to move between, various modes of speaking and being. If we wish to positively transform our world, we will need to work with a wide variety of people, even those who seem incredibly different from ourselves. Barriers need to be broken. And the type of thinking modeled by comedy can help.

A rigid insistence on a single viewpoint can block the more expansive perspective that both jokes and free societies require. Greek, Shakespearian, and other classical tragedies have repeatedly attempted to teach us the dangers of hubristic myopia, yet we refuse to learn. As the poet Frank Bidart said of *King Lear* in an interview:

> King Lear, when he's in power, can't see a damn thing. Everybody sucks up to him, and when people don't suck up to him—when Cordelia doesn't suck up to him—he can't stand it. It's very hard to see anything when you're on top. People

who can see how things are really ordered—they're perhaps always a little outside it, or started as its victim; they can see the grinding beneath what may appear a smooth surface.[83]

In *King Lear*, the Fool criticizes the King when no one else is able. After the elderly Lear banishes Cordelia, the only daughter he should have trusted, and divides his kingdom between the other two, he finds himself a disempowered figurehead. No one but the Fool is willing or able to call the King foolish. When he does, Lear is stunned by the Fool's bluntness. Lear asks, "Does thou call me a fool, boy?" The Fool responds, "All thy other titles thou hast given away; that thou wast born with."[84]

But we are not necessarily doomed to the type of foolishness Lear commits and the Fool criticizes. A comedic mindset can help us move from self-centered to multi-centered worldviews, can increase our understanding and tolerance for one another, and can teach us to develop and accept the widest possible range of non-harmful behaviors. Comedy can increase our sensitivity to the plights and pains of unfamiliar people, make it ever more difficult to marginalize and persecute other human beings, and allow us all to work together more effectively. A little more "foolishness" could make us all a lot wiser.

In addition, and as will be shown in more detail later, comedy is the purest example of how human creativity works. When two seemingly unrelated planes of thought are shown to intersect at an unforeseen point, the result could just as easily be laughter as insight. Comedic thinking can generate new ideas or even complete paradigm shifts with just a few well-chosen words. We can play various modes of being off one another, generating new ideas like a comedian creates punch lines—finding unforeseen points of intersection between seemingly unrelated things.

A Few Important Rejoinders

1. Wait, what do we mean by "democracy"?

Before we move into our actual discussion about comedy, democracy, and the creation of a free society, there are a few caveats to cover. First, it seems important to mention that the "democracy" alluded to throughout this essay is much more than just acting as "constituents" within a representative framework. The democracy this essay champions is not the democracy we currently have, but the democracy of as-yet-non-existent political arrangements that will facilitate ever-greater freedom, and will actually respect the diversity of human needs, experiences, and abilities.

Truly free institutions are *peopled* institutions, in which unique individuals share common ground on a person-to-person basis. There is no state, law, proclamation, or decree that could grant us this type of democracy. It can only be collectively constructed through arduous political processes and difficult dialogues. We can put the process in motion, but the end result will emerge and evolve in unexpected ways—like a good joke on its way to the punchline.

Democracy was not established once and for all in the late 1700s. It is an ongoing experiment under continual development. Utopia is a moving target. Perhaps surprisingly, some would disagree. In the United States, there exists a segment of the judiciary referred to as "strict constructionists." Most often associated with the late Supreme Court Justice Antonin Scalia, strict constructionists espouse total fidelity to the original intended meanings of constitutions and laws, in his case, the U.S. Constitution. In a way, strict constructionists seek to freeze our political practices at the moment they were imagined.

But throughout history, this rigid stance has been questioned by more progressive politicians. Most famously, in the midst of the U.S. Civil War, Abraham Lincoln delivered his "Gettysburg Address." Compromises written into the U.S. Constitution, such as making legal determinations as to what fraction of a human being a slave should count—not to mention even *allowing slavery in the first place*—had resulted in the sectional strife that led to the Civil War. With his "Gettysburg Address," claims Garry Wills:

> [Lincoln] performed one of the most daring acts of open-air sleight-of-hand ever witnessed by the unsuspecting. Everyone in that vast throng of thousands was having his or her intellectual pocket picked. The crowd departed with a new thing in its ideological luggage, that new constitution Lincoln had substituted for the one they brought with them.[85]

Lincoln "altered the document from within, by appeal from its letter to its spirit, subtly changing the recalcitrant stuff of that legal compromise, bringing it to its own indictment."[86] And he did so in a mere 272 words.

In the "Gettysburg Address," Lincoln declares that the United States had been founded on the notion that "all men are created equal"—here actually harkening back to the

Declaration of Independence rather than the Constitution itself. He then goes on to state that the living must carry on the "unfinished work" of those being buried at Gettysburg, and see to it that the nation shall have a "new birth of freedom."

Lincoln recognized that democracy is an ongoing experiment. Slavish dedication to dated documents will do us little good. We must always be prepared, like Lincoln, to rethink our political practices. And just as Lincoln saw in the 1860s that the political practices of the 1770s needed revising, we too can forge ahead into further births of freedom by continually developing the unfinished work of democracy. As Walt Whitman (in a way, the patron saint of these pages) wrote of democracy in 1871:

> It is a great word, whose history, I suppose, remains unwritten, because that history has yet to be enacted.[87]

And although over a century has passed since Whitman wrote these words, true democracy does not yet exist. And it may be many more centuries in the making. But working toward its realization is among the most important tasks we face.

2. Wait, what's a "revolution" and why should it be "hilarious"?

Here's our second rejoinder. Although this essay is entitled "The Revolution Will Be Hilarious," just what a "revolution" can be, and who might be a revolutionary, should be clarified. The somewhat clichéd image of the bomb-wielding revolutionary with a furrowed brow is not the image of someone who thinks much of anything is "hilarious." To this person, the revolution is most definitely a sober and unsmiling affair. But any new social order worth inhabiting will be built on increased joy and happiness. The revolution will be full of laughs and smiles or we should not bother having it at all. Or, to quote a popular misquotation of Emma Goldman, "If I can't dance, I don't want to be in your revolution."[88]

Even our most serious problems (or *especially* our most serious problems) can best be solved by implementing the attitude of openness humor makes possible. An insistence on seriousness and solemnity almost always serves pretension and pomposity, and narrows the wider perspective that comedy and free societies require. It always seems to be those whose authority is the most arbitrary and absurd who insist on being surrounded by seriousness. They fear a joke may puncture the aura of importance they have created. Distrust anyone who distrusts laughter.

In addition, relinquishing our self-serious pomposity can, perhaps surprisingly, facilitate truly serious work. As Vaclav Havel stated:

> If you don't want to dissolve in your own seriousness to the point where you become ridiculous to everyone, you must have a healthy awareness of your own human ridiculousness and nothingness. As a matter of fact, the more serious what you are doing is, the more important it becomes not to lose this awareness. If you lose this, your own actions—paradoxically— lose their seriousness. A human action becomes genuinely important when it springs from the soil of a clear sighted awareness of the temporality and ephemerality of everything human. It is only this awareness that can breathe any greatness into an action.[89]

Moreover, our imagined revolutionary with all the bombs is not only acting out of self-serious anger, but perhaps angry isolation as well. Closed cells of revolutionaries publishing pamphlets to one another in their own special jargon are in a poor position to produce truly broad and effective change. We need movements that continuously grow. This will require removing the barriers between our small, isolated worlds, so we can get together and work together. Comedic thinking is essential for this task. The revolution will certainly be hilarious. Otherwise, it will be a total joke.

3. Wait, aren't jokes cruel sometimes?

And this brings us to our final rejoinder. Although the psychology of comedic thought is essentially the same as the psychology of democratic thought, humor, in its application, can be used positively or negatively. Comedic thinking may be quite similar to democratic thinking, but comedy is not inherently democratic. Insults, mean-spirited mockery, misogynistic and racist humor can all reinforce many narrow-minded notions and make others feel less welcome. Jokes are often directed *at* someone, and are commonly used to exert or gain power in a social hierarchy.

But comedy can just as easily make others feel *less* alone, whether by helping us see one another from new perspectives, or helping us laugh at the absurdities of our common plight. There is humor that unifies and humor that tears apart. There is humor that exposes hypocrisy and humor that mocks the marginalized. Humor is not always a force for progress. It matters how we use it.

As Garry Trudeau writes in "The Abuse of Satire":

> Satire punches up, against authority of all kinds, the little guy against the powerful. Great French satirists like Molière and Daumier always punched up, holding up the self-satisfied to ridicule. Ridiculing the non-privileged is almost never funny—it's just mean.[90]

Trudeau made these remarks in reaction to the January 2015 mass shooting at the offices of the satirical weekly *Charlie Hebdo* in Paris. The magazine had angered a large swath of the Islamic world by publishing cartoons depicting the prophet Muhammad. Or that's the popular narrative. But a quick perusal of the issues of *Charlie Hebdo* from the months preceding the attack show far fewer instances of actual religious satire in comparison to mean-spirited caricatures of Muslim immigrants. For the most part, *Charlie Hebdo* punched down, and mocked the already marginalized. Although this mass shooting was (obviously) horrific, *Charlie Hebdo* is not exactly the noblest use of free speech. Just because you're a martyr doesn't mean you were right. And just because your jokes are pissing people off, that doesn't necessarily mean you're pushing hard truths or something. Je ne suis pas Charlie.

While *Charlie Hebdo* definitely punched downward, antisemitism, which also isn't funny, is based on a *perceived* upward punch. Since Jews are rumored to run the banks, the media, and Hollywood, it is assumed that they secretly run the world. These sorts of conspiracies have roots older than movies or any currently bankable currency—contemporary antisemitism is just new seeds sprouting from the same old shit. So antisemetic punches aren't actually aimed up or down. They're more like punches thrown by a blind guy on LSD trying to hit his hallucinations. It would almost be sad if it didn't cause so much harm.

Satire and other kinds of comedy are best when they attack the citadels of power. When the powerless are attacked, or when punches are thrown randomly based on erroneous information, jokes can be destructive and awful. Luckily, it's not really the *practice* of comedy, but the *psychology* of comedy with which this essay is concerned. But because we will need to at least periodically touch on the practice of comedy, for the sake of clarity, I will call comedy that mocks the pompous and encourages creative thinking and increased understanding *progressive humor*, and comedy that attacks the marginalized or reinforces stereotypes and ossified thinking *regressive humor*.

Alright, we're ready to discuss how comedy works.

So Here's How Comedy Works

In *The Act of Creation*, Arthur Koestler analyzes creativity, and demonstrates that the same principles of creation apply for everyone from the Jester, to the Scientist and the Sage.[91] He claims that his book "proposes a theory of the act of creation—of the conscious and unconscious processes underlying scientific discovery, artistic originality, and comic inspiration. It endeavors to show that all creative activities have a basic pattern in common, and to outline that pattern."[92] He begins with humor, and shows that it is the bisociation of two seemingly separate planes of thought or matrices of action at an unexpected point that makes jokes (and other "eureka!" moments) work. As Koestler states, "I have coined the term 'bisociation' in order to make a distinction between the routine skills of thinking on a single 'plane,' as it were, and the creative act, which, as I shall try to show, always operates on more than one plane."[93] Bisociative acts, found most obviously in humor, are present in all acts of creation.

How does bisociation function? Not much makes a joke unfunny quite like explaining it, but here are some examples and explanations anyway.

> A ham sandwich walks into a bar. The bartender says, "Hey, we don't serve food here!"

In this joke, two senses of the word "serve" are played off one another.

Then there's this:

> Q: What's the difference between space pirates and clinical depression?
>
> A: I don't battle space pirates every day!

Or here's one from Groucho Marx:

> One morning I shot an elephant in my pajamas. How he got in my pajamas I'll never know.

Each of these jokes works when an unexpected point of connection is created between two seemingly distinct ideas—what Koestler would call a "bisociation."

What is going on in these moments of bisociation? In his *Philosophical Investigations*, Ludwig Wittgenstein—a notoriously humorless man who once claimed that a very good philosophical work could be written consisting entirely of jokes—discusses our perception of indefinite drawings like this duck-rabbit:

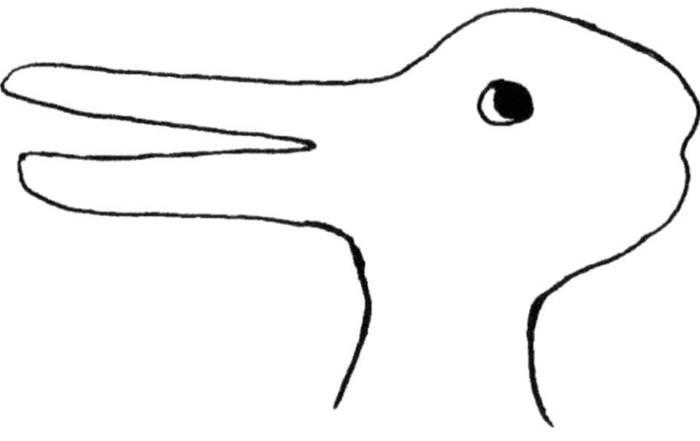

At one moment, we may perceive this picture as a duck, but a moment later, see it as a rabbit. What happens in these instants when the duck becomes a rabbit or the rabbit becomes a duck? The picture does not change, but our perception of it does. And our perception shifts in a very similar manner when "in my pajamas" becomes "in my pajamas."

So that's "bisociation." And although it is a useful term, it requires some expansion. The binary logic of bisociation oversimplifies the true complexities of many jokes and other creative thoughts. "Multisociation" is preferable. Moshé Feldenkrais argued that any actual choice requires more than two options. Rather than going back and forth between just this or that, a third option (or more) introduces a higher level of nuance, and truly choosing becomes a possibility. Similarly, both rich experiences and funny jokes usually operate on more than two levels. Increased elements yield increased nuance, which yields increased usefulness.

We can clarify and expand on multisociation by bringing in the Russian linguist Mikhail Bakhtin's related notions of "heteroglossia" and the "hybrid construction," although he, like Koestler, usually writes of binaries between just two elements. Heteroglossia, as defined by Bakhtin, is the coexistence of various sub-vocabularies within a single linguistic code. Heteroglossia is all about the importance of context over text. Every utterance any human ever makes bears the mark of a time, place, social class, generation, or ideology. Language cannot be neutral.

Heteroglossia comes into comedy in "hybrid constructions." These occur in passages and utterances that employ a single speaker, but multiple vocabularies simultaneously. As Bakhtin states:

What we are calling a hybrid construction is an utterance that belongs, by its grammatical (syntactic) and compositional markers, to a single speaker, but that actually contains mixed within it two utterances, two speech manners, two styles, two "languages," two semantic and axiological belief systems. We repeat, there is no formal—compositional and syntactic—boundary between these utterances, styles, languages, belief systems; the division of voices and languages takes place within the limits of a single syntactic whole, often within the limits of a simple sentence.[94]

In other words, a single word or statement can be a duck, a rabbit, or just some lines on paper, depending on how we look at it. Or, to combine Koestler and Bakhtin, it is the multisociation of multiple non-neutral linguistic codes that yields hybrid constructions—and comedy. In humor, two or more self-consistent and seemingly incompatible planes of thought intersect at an unforeseen point. Effective punch lines are logical, but unexpected.

What's So Funny About Peace, Love, and Understanding?

Humor and creativity require the ability to see the world from multiple perspectives—a skill equally important in behaving democratically. In order to either make jokes or communicate effectively with people outside one's immediate circle, one must have an understanding of, and an ability to move between, various modes of speaking and being. Jokes require understanding and utilizing difference for comedic effect. Democracies require understanding, coexisting, and cooperating with that same difference. (And although we should never cease attempting to understand others, we should also recognize that others will always remain others. Actual experience is nontransferable.)

In order to effectively explore the corollaries between comedy and democracy, we will need to do some hopefully not too confusing hopping between the related issues of self-perception, other-perception, stereotypes, outsider-hood, and language. I am going to try to keep it all concise and organized, but sadly, we have officially reached the part of this essay where the complexities of the world slam into the attempted tidiness of the printed page and make maintaining clarity increasingly difficult. So keep rooting for me and we'll get through this together.

On his *WTF Podcast*, Marc Maron interviews various comedians about their lives, their craft, and the social functions of funniness. In episode 224 of the *WTF Podcast*, Maron interviewed the black comedian and actor Chris Rock, who discussed pitching sketch ideas to the white writers at *Saturday Night Live*. White comedians, he argued, had a distinct advantage.

> Because they share a culture—they have kinda the same moms, kinda the same dads, they grew up in the same environment— there's a shorthand that happens. They get the little things about you that make you funny. And when you're the black guy, no one gets the little things. They just get the hits.[95]

The details of black culture escaped *Saturday Night Live*'s white writers. It made them miss the nuances of Rock's jokes—the sorts of subtleties they would be able to perceive in white comedians. This does not make them racist. It simply means that the details of black culture were not part of their mental makeup.

The process for better comprehending Rock's jokes and the process for rendering him less of an "other" are basically the same. Learning why someone is funny happens through learning why that someone is also a fellow, suffering human being. The path to tolerance and the path to laughter are identical. Discovering the details of an unfamiliar someone's plight and pain will reveal the reasons for their laughter. And make it harder to add to their pain.

Comedy requires the simultaneous use of various vocabularies. We don't just need to *understand* the nuances of various cultures, we need to *do something interesting* with those nuances. Here's an example: Comedy Central named Richard Pryor the greatest stand-up comedian of all time. Besides his obvious skills as a comedian and his ability to present his immense personal pain and suffering honestly and universally, the perspective he had as a member of a marginalized minority in the United States who *simultaneously* operated within the context of mainstream culture gave him a unique frame of reference, allowing him to play black and white culture off one another in interesting and unexpected ways. Someone who exists solely as a member of a single culture is less likely to see that culture from the outside and realize what's so funny about it. Its practices are likely to remain unquestioned, while those of other cultures will seem strange or unnatural. The smooth surface is visible, but not the grinding beneath it.

Pryor's simultaneous existence in two cultures gave him distance on both, making him particularly demonstrative of W.E.B. Dubois' notion of African American double consciousness—a split caused by living the American experience with an African heritage. Pryor's dual cultural consciousness, coupled with his ability to find funny connections between these cultures, contributed immensely to his success.

Although Pryor pointed out difference, his work was not divisive. Instead, he emphasized the common humanity that transcends difference. As he states,

> My comedy was colorblind. None of it would've worked if the world was all one color. I mean, even black ain't beautiful if it's the only color you look at every day. Life's richness, its beauty and excitement, comes from the diversity of things.[96]

Why play up difference to be divisive? "We're all people, you know? That's hard enough."[97]

Even when skilled comedians are not members of minority groups, they still tend to be marginalized outsiders. The beautiful and popular kids rarely grow up to be professional comedians. Or even funny for that matter. And this is most likely due to the lack of an outside perspective that comes from one's easy acceptance into a dominant culture. In episode 163 of the *WTF Podcast*, Maron spoke with the late-night talk-show host Conan O'Brien. O'Brien, after discussing his nerdy, awkward childhood, stated,

> I'm always suspicious if I think a comedian's too good looking, and they were a great athlete when they were young. I almost can't believe that they're going to be any good. […] I'll have some really good looking intern on the show, who tells me that he's also a great athlete or something, and he'll say, "Yeah, I'm thinking of going into stand-up." And I just want to say, "No, no, no. This is for *us*. This is our consolation prize."[98]

Ostracized outcasts usually create the best comedy. They spend most of their lives seeing the world from the outside, viewing it from a perspective that those wrapped comfortably in its machinations cannot. It is impossible to comment on a system one cannot even perceive *as a system*, that one simply perceives as "reality." But when a dominant culture makes you an "other," it becomes possible to see it for what it actually is—just another historically contingent culture in the shifting tapestry of time. We *all* need to step outside the machinations of our ingrained patterns of thought and action and see where our various self-consistent (or inconsistent) modes of being do (or don't) intersect, so that we can be more tolerant, less cruel, and increasingly democratic.

On Funny Women

Of course, the long-standing lack of women comedians complicates my argument about outside perspectives and the creation of comedy. The notion that existing as an outsider within a dominant culture gives one an advantage in being funny should make women comedians incredibly common. This finally seems to be changing, or at least starting to change, but women comedians remain both rare and distinctly *women* comedians.

Perhaps surprisingly, "Why aren't women funny?" is an even older question than the people who usually pose it. In an essay entitled "Why Aren't Women Funny?," Christopher Hitchens attempts to explain this startlingly common sentiment. Although he sets out to prove that there is something inherently unfunny about women, his evidence and his thesis never quite come together. By failing, his essay inadvertently uncovers some interesting points. What he *actually* demonstrates is not that women are somehow congenitally less funny than men, but that many men are threatened by funny women, creating an unspoken social practice wherein most women keep their jokes to themselves in the company of other genders.

Because humor requires exceptional intelligence and the ability to stay ahead of an audience, a woman who is funnier than a man also seems smarter. This can be threatening to many men. They do, after all, believe it's their world. James Brown told them so. As Hitchens writes, "Precisely because humor is a sign of intelligence (and many women believe, or were taught by their mothers, that they become threatening to men if they appear too bright), it could be that in some way men do not *want* women to be funny. They want them as an audience, not as rivals."[99]

But beyond the subtle social practices that make it difficult for women to be funny around men, the standard stereotypes and stock characters that comprise much of comedy's (and the world's) content typically come from a very male perspective. As the female cartoonist Betty Swords—who began publishing her cartoons in the mid-1950s—said of the depiction of women in most comics:

> Women were dumb about money, dumb about driving, dumb about anything that happened in the real world. And that began my trip into feminism. I began to see how humor treated women. Dumb, dumb, dumb.[100]

In other words, women usually are the joke, not the makers of jokes. In his essay "Feminism and Pragmatism," Richard Rorty states that "most oppressors have had the wit to teach the oppressed a language in which the oppressed will sound crazy—*even to themselves*—if they describe themselves *as* oppressed."[101]

Progressive humor can make us see things in new ways, while *regressive* humor can make us see things in the same over-simplified ways again and again. We need to expand the depth and breadth of materials we use. In her book *Humor Power*, Swords states:

> The male images of women created by cartoonists were accepted as the truth about women. For example: The woman driver is the safest driver, according to the National Safety Council—but not to the National Cartoonists Society. To them, she's the quintessential "dumb driver," an idea so set in the concrete of comic tradition that it's become humor shorthand: when we see a cartoon of a woman driver, we know automatically that she's a dumb driver. Just ask a man which he believes, the Cartoonists Society or the Safety Council?[102]

Humor can reinforce ugly and regressive stereotypes or it can subvert them. So we don't just need to tell funnier jokes. We also need to pay attention to the sorts of jokes we tell. We need *progressive*, not *regressive humor*.

It's worth pointing out that there are interesting examples of women who attacked standard misogynistic stereotypes with a form of comedic jujitsu—using the weight of our culture's asinine assumptions to topple those very assumptions—and achieved mass cultural success in the process. On *I Love Lucy*, still one of the funniest shows in the history of television, Lucille Ball played "Lucy Ricardo," a ditzy housewife who—as cultural expectations would dictate—kept her real age and hair color a secret, and was (of course) terrible with money. By performing *as* what we expected to see, Ball was able to play *with* our expectations. She overplayed Lucy Ricardo's stereotyped characteristics to such an extent that she revealed them to be the hollow absurdities they are. So although stereotypes typically fuel reactionary thinking, they can sometimes be used to undercut themselves.

However useful and interesting such cultural practices may be, simply exposing sexist suppositions is just a preliminary step in the liberation of women. A society's dominant voices determine that society's terms of engagement, and female perspectives have been marginalized. As Simone de Beauvoir writes in *The Second Sex*, woman currently "knows and chooses herself not as she exists for herself but as man defines her."[103] Women's (and other dominated or marginalized groups') languages, vocabularies, and modes of being are often prevented from fully developing. To quote Beauvoir again,

> Woman is not a fixed reality but a becoming; she has to be compared with man in her becoming; that is, her *possibilities* have to be defined: what skews the issues so much is that she is being reduced to what she was, to what she is today, while the question concerns her capacities; the fact is that her capacities manifest themselves clearly only when they have been realized.[104]

The realization of a still-nascent truth can counter a dominant truth, give us new ways to interact, and new jokes to tell. The creation and de-marginalization of a truly feminine vocabulary is needed for women to have a real voice—comic or otherwise—in society. A dominated culture does not have the freedom to be itself. So in a weird sort of way, "woman" is not yet the name of an actualized entity. Only when the yoke of cultural dominance has been sloughed off once and for all can "woman" become the name of a being with a distinct and recognizable vocabulary—a vocabulary defined by what it *is*, rather than what it *is not*.

Hysterical Contingencies and Comedic Vistas

Obviously, based on much of what has been said above, understanding language is essential for understanding democracy. Jokes regularly require subtle (and-not-so-subtle) manipulations of language and vocabularies, while democracies require the ability to understand and communicate effectively with "others."

In his essay "Authority and American Usage," David Foster Wallace points out that a child who can only speak "correct" English is

> actually in the same dialectical position as the class's "slow" kid who can't learn to stop using *ain't* and *bringed*. Exactly the same position. One is punished in class, the other on the playground, but both are deficient in the same linguistic skill—viz., the ability to move between various dialects and levels of "correctness," the ability to communicate one way with peers

and another way with teachers and another with families and another with T-ball coaches and so on.[105]

Or, as Mikhail Bakhtin states a little less informally in "Discourse in the Novel,"

> Consciousness finds itself inevitably facing the necessity of *having to choose a language*. With each literary-verbal performance, consciousness must actively orient itself amidst heteroglossia, it must move in and occupy a position for itself within it, it chooses, in other words, a "language."[106]

Behaving democratically and making jokes often require the ability to simultaneously utilize several systems of discourse. If one doesn't understand the differences in communication styles between peers, parents, and T-ball coaches, one will not be able to crack jokes about or between these groups. Nor will one be able to comfortably coexist with them. Comedy, democracy, and language are all closely related.

Ludwig Wittgenstein, whom you may remember from the duck-rabbit drawing, managed to revolutionize the philosophy of language not just once, but twice in the twentieth century. And when he did it the second time, he was definitely on to something. The first time Wittgenstein revolutionized the philosophy of language, he worked within the parameters set by Gottlob Frege and Bertrand Russell. Like these thinkers, the young Wittgenstein sought foundations for language and mathematics. His *Tractatus Logico-Philosophicus*, the only philosophical work he published in his lifetime, analyzes true/false assertoric statements, and declares, among other things, that only these types of statements have sense. A statement that cannot be declared true or false is senseless, and the subject should be passed over in silence.

But over the course of the next several decades, Wittgenstein came to reject just about everything Frege, Russell, and his younger self had said. Wittgenstein's later work entirely jettisons the notion that language and math have foundations at all. Rather, he suggests, humans develop various systems of rules, and then follow, ignore, or change those rules. Meaning is determined by use. Our languages and mathematical systems are not descriptions of reality, but tools for navigating the world.

If we teach a child the name of an object, maybe a car or a desk, and then say the name of that object to the child, who in turn brings it to us, has the child learned a proposition that can be true or false? No. The child has learned a system of rules for a specific linguistic situation. This system of rules is not made meaningful by the truth or falsity of its propositions, but by *the use* to which it can be put. The way a vocabulary operates in the world is what makes it meaningful.

Frege, Russell, and the young Wittgenstein all declared logic to be language's quasi-metaphysical foundation, and then attempted to use logic to explain language. But logic is not an *explanation* of language, just a re-description of it in different terms. In fact, there *are no* meta-theories of language, just accounts of the various ways languages are used.

Wittgenstein's earlier work only analyzed text, but with his later work, he came to accept (and emphasize) the incredible importance of context. Meaning is not "discovered" by finding a language that corresponds to reality, but by creating better tools for navigating the world. And just as we wouldn't argue whether a hammer or some other tool is "true" or "corresponds to reality," we should evaluate vocabularies by their function and usefulness. Do they allow us to deal with the world effectively? If they do, they are useful and worth keeping. If not, we should abandon them.

The Western capitalist description of the world is a worn-out tool that needs to be replaced. It describes the world as one of endless competition, and encourages the current rage for selfishness that, if left unchecked, will be our undoing. The apostles of this worldview not only demand compliance with their commands, but total adoption of their values. As Thomas Merton writes of the young Gandhi:

> He had to a great extent renounced the beliefs, the traditions, the habits of thought, of India. He spoke, thought, and acted like an Englishman, except of course that an Englishman was precisely what he could never, by any miracle, become. He was an alienated Asian whose sole function in life was to be perfectly English without being English at all: to prove the superiority of the West by betraying his own heritage and his own self, thinking as a white man without ceasing to be "a Nigger."[107]

Compliance with capitalism is often made necessary for survival. In South Africa in the late 1800s, the English faced a labor shortage in the mines, mainly because the natives preferred not to perform such miserable work, and stayed on their farms instead. So in 1894, the English government passed the Glen Grey Act, creating a labor tax that had to be paid in shillings. And those shillings had to be earned. Either work in the mines or go to jail. Most coercion into the economic system is less overt than this, but it is no less coercive.

The imperialist West adopted the hubristic attitude that the non-European cultures that conquest crushed had been stalled societies awaiting the blessings of "civilization" and "free markets." Victory appeared to bring vindication. But with germ warfare, nuclear weapons, and the total degradation of the planet through institutionalized selfishness as the West's most notable "achievements," it may be time to accept that many of the cultures that have been destroyed and dispatched to the academic ghetto of anthropology journals often offer more elegant social forms, sensibilities, and ways of being.

In Detroit, Michigan, an African American artist named Dabls has built an enormous outdoor installation entitled "Iron Teaching Rocks How To Rust." Old paint cans and piles of rebar try to teach rocks and chunks of concrete how to rust like them. It looks like a classroom—the iron up front, the rocks lined up in chairs. The iron embodies Western imperialist attempts to bring the glories of rapid self-destruction to those who could actually sustain themselves.

In the film *Embrace of the Serpent,* a shaman from a nearly-vanished tribe in Colombia leads two separate Western explorers on two separate trips to find one medicinal plant. Antonio Bolívar Salvador plays the shaman Karamakate, the last of his tribe. But the reality is not very different from the fiction. Ninety percent of the indigenous people of Colombia have been wiped out. The herbicide glyphosate, applied liberally to coca crops, is causing cancer and birth defects. Environmental degradation and violent imperialism are making life impossible. As the film's director, Ciro Guerra, stated, "These are people who have managed to live in the same place for 10,000 years without overpopulating it, without polluting it, without destroying its resources."[108] Then the lessons of just how to rust were taught with all the force that could be brought to bear. Now the classroom is a mess and the school is burning down.

The worldview this essay espouses is so different from the currently dominant capitalist one that it is alarming. Free societies require tolerance, understanding, cooperation, and mutual aid—not the competitive, accumulative, and commercial values encouraged by the market economy. Without radical change—both personally and politically— the only future we can look forward to is one of ever-mounting credit card debt and oceans at a rolling boil. We cannot go on wasting resources and destroying land. We need to maintain what we have so that life on Earth can continue.

At this point in history, it almost seems beyond debate that our social, political, and economic systems are fueling the destruction of our planet. The capitalist demand for endless growth and ever-increasing consumption in a world with finite resources is quite obviously suicidal. And the governmental defense of this economic system—creating laws that make capitalist economic practices ever more official and entrenched—institutionalizes and perpetuates our self-destructive greed.

Comedy, Creativity, and the Shock of the New

It is important that we synthesize, bisociate, and multisociate all our assorted worldviews together to create new vocabularies and new ideas. The old ideas have failed us, but a comedic mindset can help us create new ones. As has been mentioned, comedy is creativity in its purest form. Comedy not only requires *seeing* from multiple perspectives, but *doing* something clever with those perspectives. Punch lines possess the same structure as both artistic creation and scientific discovery. This is probably why Wittgenstein thought a book of philosophy could be written consisting entirely of jokes. Humor works through the multisociation of seemingly separate planes at unforeseen points. A punch line is only funny if it is surprising. If people "see it coming," the joke will fail.

This is why humor often ages poorly. As David Berman writes in his collection of poems, *Actual Air*:

> It seems our comedy dates the quickest.
> If you laugh out loud at Shakespeare's jokes,
> I hope you won't be insulted
> if I say you're trying too hard.
> Even sketches from the original Saturday Night Live
> seem slow witted and obvious now.[109]

Once a new way of seeing has been introduced, the surprise needed to generate laughter is gone. In both humor and scientific discovery, two seemingly unrelated planes are found to intersect at an unexpected point. And just as the Copernican revolution has ceased to be mind-blowing, most older humor now seems stilted and predictable. Comedy perpetually requires new multisociations to stay surprising and funny. Humor tends toward newness, just as our ideas should.

Moreover, just being *exposed* to comedy can increase our creativity. The psychologist Alice M. Isen conducted a study in which college students were given a book of matches, a box of tacks, and a candle. They were then asked to affix the candle to a corkboard in such a way that the candle would burn without dripping wax on the floor. Students who were shown a comedy film beforehand had a 75% success rate. Those who were shown a film about mathematics figured it out 20% of the time, while those who watched nothing had a 13% success rate.[110]

Isen then conducted a supplementary experiment in which an additional group were given candy bars before attempting the challenge. Comedy still conquered all. As Isen states, "Contrary to expectation, subjects in the gift condition did not show improved performance as those in the comedy-film condition did. Thus it may be specifically humor, and not positive affect more generally, that gives rise to improved creative problem solving."[111] In short, comedy can prepare our minds for creative thinking and seeing things from fresh perspectives.

This makes etymological sense as well. The word "humor" comes from the Latin *umor*, for bodily fluid, which entered Old French (still meaning bodily fluid) as *humor*. In English, the word retains implications of fluidity and the ability to flow with changing circumstances, with the shift in meaning from bodily fluids to jokes pivoting on the medieval and

Renaissance belief that shifting "humors" are responsible for shifts in temperament.[112]

Creating the Future

Comedic thinking involves flowing and changing creatively in relation to obstacles and encounters, and this fluidity of being can help us create a better world. The future remains unwritten. No template from the past can tell us what we ought to do. We can look back and find inspiration, but what we really need are new social forms and new individuals of never-before-seen varieties. Our ossified and outmoded forms need to be disassembled and reconfigured.

Although we cannot just will the unforeseen into existence, we can create the circumstances where it can emerge. If we guarantee collective, free inquiry, we create the possibility for beliefs and worldviews to collide and combine. There are no rules for this collision and combination beyond simply guaranteeing that freedom. Just as good punchlines are surprising, new ideas arise from unforeseen combinations. Nothing new comes from thinking old thoughts over and over again.

But, sadly enough, not everyone wants wide varieties of worldviews inhabiting the same spaces. Jared Taylor, a Yale-educated white supremacist who prefers being called a "racial realist," argues that monolithic cultures of single races are more stable, and therefore preferable, to multicultural societies, with Japan as his prime example. "Stability" may sound good, but in Taylor's case, "stability" is both a cover for racism and the manifestation of an intense fear of change.

New ideas and new forms will not arise if separate cultures separately maintain their separate ways. By wearing a suit and hosting conferences, he and his followers present a slightly more respectable version of racist thought than a bunch of drunken skinheads, but the ideas motivating them aren't much different.

In January 2016, as Donald Trump launched his campaign for the U.S. Presidency by demanding a wall along the U.S.-Mexico border and threatening to ban Muslims from entering the United States, Taylor helped make a pre-recorded "robocall" urging the people of Iowa to support Trump. He closed his statement by saying, "We don't need Muslims. We need smart, well-educated white people who will assimilate to our culture. Vote Trump."[113] But we don't need assimilation. We need interpenetration.

It is only through total freedom of thought and the acceptance of all non-harmful behaviors that we can create the circumstances for a better world to emerge. Of course, the sort of optimism that would believe a better world is even possible has gone horribly out of style. The future is not what it used to be. The Utopian visions of the nineteenth and twentieth centuries have given way to dystopian dread. In the Middle Ages, the world was seen as a temporary stopping place where humanity suffered for a bit while awaiting final judgment. To the medieval mind, perfection existed before the fall and would only come again after the apocalypse. But following the Enlightenment, and particularly for many nineteenth and twentieth century artists and radicals, perfection became an Earthly possibility.

Marxist and Modernist thought, as well as Utopian novels like William Morris' *News from Nowhere*, Edward Bellamy's *Looking Backward,* and Upton Sinclair's *The Millenium,* all exemplify the once-common belief in the possibility of a better future. But as we made our way into a new millennium, we forgot to bring such hopes with us. If the future is imagined at all, it is almost invariably a bleak one, with films like *Blade Runner, Mad Max, Wall-E,* and *The Road* exemplifying the common notion that the future, if we have one, will not be pretty. We are now left with neither God nor Utopia—stalled in place as we await our inevitable collapse.

We can no longer afford to do without Utopian thinking. If we don't dream big now, there won't be anyone left to dream at all. To do so, we must first learn to embrace complexity, rather than taking the easy path and mentally foisting a false homogeneity onto an intricate and multifaceted world. A free society functions when unique individuals share common ground. The type of thinking exemplified by comedy is exactly the type of thinking we need to master if we wish to reimagine the future. Comedy can help us see how to think and speak on multiple planes simultaneously, and to multisociate and synthesize all our various worldviews together to create new ideas and new vocabularies—which we could then multisociate, on and on, into a future we cannot yet imagine.

We should respect—and even revel in—our incredible diversity of individual needs and skills, while still cooperating and functioning as communities. In *The Ecology of Freedom,* Murray Bookchin calls for an "ethics of complementarity." He points out that a self is "nourished by variety," and cannot thrive if it guards itself against "threatening, invasive otherness."[114] The freedom afforded by such an "equality of unequals" would help us respect—and even revel in—our incredible diversity of needs and skills.

In the first paragraph of *Democratic Vistas*, Walt Whitman claims that what is needed for true liberty is first, "a large variety of character," and second, "full play for human nature to expand itself in numberless and even *conflicting* directions."[115] I italicized "conflicting" for a reason. Whitman is demanding much more than diversity through preservation and protection. It seems essential to emphasize that this essay is not a call for the kind, gentle acceptance of every imaginable idea. Truth may be historically contingent, and our vocabularies may "merely" be tools, but there are better and worse ways to describe the world. Some vocabularies are actually quite harmful, and, as has been pointed out, the currently dominant one is particularly so.

But this "conflict" between worldviews does not need to involve bashing heads to beat new ideas into them. Rather, we can create and actualize better ways of being that will turn our world based on greed into another embarrassing relic of the past. Writing and whining about it like this is not enough. We shouldn't be content to simply complain that the capitalist class is raping and pillaging our planet. Why should we expect them to stop if we can't present something better? The problem isn't so much their success as it is our failure.

In order to supplant what is, we will need new vocabularies, and the type of thinking modeled by comedy can help. An act of quasi-comedic multisociation can produce an idea or object that has no place in the world. By introducing something that doesn't belong within our existing systems, moments of multisociative insight can disrupt the machinations of the given and expand the scope of the possible. There is a war of vocabularies to be waged, and for now, the capitalist notion of life as a quest for profit has set our terms of engagement. But these terms can be called into question in radical and fundamental ways.

It may be difficult, but we *can* multisociatively recreate the spaces we inhabit, whether they are physical, mental, literary, or even dream space. Like our languages, our methods of dissecting, dividing, and dealing with reality are just tools for navigating the world. We can reinvent any of them. Actually, we *must* reinvent them. Nothing less than the future of humanity is incumbent on these acts of multisociative re-creation. Upon undertaking this task, we will find ourselves confronted with problems like creation and resistance in the face of subtle and often hidden forces of social control. Distancing ourselves from what is and moving toward what could be will require numerous acts of creation, incalculable acts of will, and the determined rejection of habit.

Space and time are necessary categories, but the shape they take is ultimately our own creation. Every social structure—past, present, and future—is a historically contingent artifice. The political and economic structures we inhabit, the divisions between spaces for work, leisure, privacy, and socializing, as well as the modes and methods available for moving between these spaces, determine the apparent limits of the possible. And the time we perceive is determined by the ways we navigate these constructed spaces. Schools, jobs, prisons, asylums, and hospitals all mold us to the machinations of capitalism. They are all part of a single system—a system set to the rhythms of the marketplace, which in turn sets *us* to the rhythms of the marketplace.

Capitalism forces humans to act as players in the game of commerce. What business wants, business gets. And what business wants are citizens whose survival is dependent on successfully playing the capitalist game—to be marketable beings who appeal to employers. We have been shaped by and for this reality. Freeing ourselves from it will not be easy.

How to Begin?

As should be obvious by now, comedy can help. We can create quasi-comedic fissures in the given by multisociating what is with what could be, using punch line-like moments of insight to punch holes in the present. We need to destroy all our archetypes, stereotypes, and other ossified symbols. They are not engaged with creatively—they just sit there, waiting to be understood. Or they are used in the same predictable ways, again and again. Their meaning already exists. They are almost always part of the given we should refuse to take. (Not coincidentally, stereotypes and archetypes typically constitute the content of the most hackneyed and predictable humor.) Truly creative multisociations, on the other hand, evoke something new.

Moments of quasi-comedic creativity can offer ruptures in reality where something truly unique and unforeseen can enter. When we comprehend where two self-consistent and apparently incompatible planes do in fact intersect, we help reshape our world.

Not everything that's funny is necessarily a joke. We need to wage, and win, a war of vocabularies.

In *Humor Power*, Betty Swords states:

> If humor has the power to shape society—and given that our society is one of growing violence and alienation—can we not alter and improve society, at least our corner of it, by changing our humor? Only when we recognize humor's power—for good as well as evil—can we control that power for positive purposes in both our personal and professional lives.[116]

Comedy can reinforce old ideas or it can create new ones. The lessons of comedy are powerful and useful. We just need to take the right lessons and use them in the right ways. As funny as it may sound, if we take the lessons of comedy seriously, our species may have a shot at survival.

The revolution will be hilarious.

Seriously.

BUY THE LAND AND BUY THE LIGHT

In 1603, Johann Bayer introduced one of the oldest star naming systems still in use. In Bayer's system, the visibly brightest star in each constellation is named Alpha, the second Beta, and so on through the Greek alphabet, giving us names like Alpha Centauri and Beta Centauri. There are other systems, such as the Henry Draper Catalog, which identifies over 300,000 stars by number. For instance, Alpha Centauri is known there as HD 125823. Betelgeuse, or Alpha Orionis, is HD 39801.

Like Betelgeuse and Alpha Centauri, many stars have multiple names. And although the International Astronomical Union recognizes most star names, even they have their limits. Their website states, "The IAU frequently receives requests from individuals who want to buy stars or name stars after other persons. Some commercial enterprises purport to offer such services for a fee. However, such 'names' have no formal or official validity whatsoever."[117]

The most well-known of the star-selling enterprises that so irks the International Astronomical Union is the International Star Registry. Founded in 1979, the Star Registry allows people to pay to name a star whatever they want. In addition to a star name, customers also receive a parchment certificate and a map with coordinates. It's quite the deal.

The Star Registry's website admits that "International Star Registry star naming is not recognized by the scientific community."[118] But the thing is, stars don't care what we call them. They don't recognize the Star Registry *or* the scientific community. There's a star in the Andromeda Constellation we could either call HD 10307 or Margaret Thatcher. It was burning back when our most advanced ancestors were single-celled organisms. It will still be burning when cockroaches inherit the Earth. And it is very, very far away. We are entirely irrelevant to this star. Beyond the bounds of Earth, neither name has any more validity than the other.

So my problem is not that the people at the International Star Registry think they can, like the International Astronomical Union, name stars. Of course they can name stars. They do it all the time. What bothers me is that they can make a successful business out of it. A world where purchasing points of light makes perfect sense, and where the International Astronomical Union "frequently receives requests from individuals who want to buy stars," is a world with its goals and values wildly misaligned. Now may be the only moment in human history when selling stars would sound anything but absurd. But what has changed? How could a business, inconceivable in any other era, survive for decades?

To answer that, we need to pivot from purchasing stars to purchasing land. Given what follows, using the Star Registry as a set-up may seem unfair. New notions of ownership that emerged in the last few centuries made the International Star Registry possible. These notions were instated through destruction and genocide, and were then used to justify further destruction and genocide. But however unfair it may seem, it was a chance encounter with the Star Registry's website that led to the rest of this research. And that initial question remains interesting. Just what happened to make such a business even possible?

The development of exclusive private property provided the context in which the Star Registry could come into being. Exclusive private property is a surprisingly recent phenomenon that emerged as Europeans, particularly the English, colonized North America. The practices that emerged as they divided and sold an entire continent—empty except for all the people living on it—ushered private property into existence, along with the new idea that anything we survey can become our own personal possession.

And as those colonizers divided that not-so-empty continent, a whole lot of surveying went on. It was a very popular profession. For example, three of the four U.S.

presidents whose faces are carved into Mount Rushmore worked as surveyors. George Washington was sixteen when he accompanied George William Fairfax on a surveying expedition in the Shenandoah Valley, becoming one of the continent's youngest professional surveyors. Thomas Jefferson served as the county surveyor of Albemarle County in 1773. His father, Peter Jefferson, had also been a surveyor. Later, after the frontier shifted from Virginia to Illinois, a young Abraham Lincoln took up the profession. "New Boston, Bath, Petersburg, and Huron were among the towns that he laid out."[119] And even if Theodore Roosevelt, that fourth face carved into Mount Rushmore, never worked as a surveyor, he still loved to see land divided and sold. He claimed that "civilization" ought to be spread by "the order-loving races of the earth doing their duty" and acquiring "the world's waste spaces."[120]

There are reasons why there were suddenly so many surveyors once the English started colonizing North America. In 1620, the same year the Mayflower set sail with some of England's earliest committed colonizers, the mathematician, geometer, and astronomer Edmund Gunter introduced Gunter's chain. Sixty-six feet long, ten of his chains by ten of his chains mark ten acres. Together with his new triangulation methods, surveying became a science. This made strict property lines possible, and allowed land to be more accurately quantified and commodified. Trespassing became an enforceable offense. In tandem with the new notions of ownership that appeared as the United States became a nation, a world emerged in which any land could become exclusively held and forcefully defended.

Exclusive private property was a new development. Although many of the English colonizers immediately and irrevocably perceived the indigenous as "savages," tribal land management along the East Coast was not remarkably different from the English feudal-era methods the colonists brought with them. Among natives along the East Coast, land was ultimately held and managed by a chief or other powerful figure, but this did not constitute "ownership" by that person, just the power to allocate resources. This person granted tribe members access to certain things at certain times of the year. Yet this was still not "ownership." Land was not "owned," just used. In addition to this rotating access to resources, there were also common areas and shared supplies.

In the English system, everything was ultimately held by the crown, and a lord or earl granted land and materials as needed. There were common areas and shared resources here as well. The English had much more of a tendency to stay put for centuries, but the indigenous people and the colonists managed their land similarly. Early New England settlements had a village green, or common area, usually just a few acres, in the center of town. There was rarely enough space for all the village livestock to graze there, but there were common pastures outside of town. "Children brought their family cow or horse to the green and left the animal in care of the town herdsman, who then led the herd to a distant piece of common ground. Late in the afternoon the herdsman returned with the livestock, and the children came to the green to fetch home their own animals."[121] Gristmills and sawmills operated as public utilities, not private businesses. Besides some common-field agriculture, there were also shared woodlands for lumber and hunting.

But when the United States seceded from England, the crown no longer owned the land. It could become anyone's. Everyone could be their own earl. This was part of an understandable attempt to undermine centuries of aristocratic control exerted by a few families. But combined with Gunter's new systems of surveying, exclusive private property came rushing into history. Lines were drawn. Trespassers were prosecuted. The commons disappeared and were soon forgotten. Rather than a shared resource outside of town, land became a commodity—one person's private possession to be bought and disposed of in any way.

And when the Fifth Amendment to the U.S. Constitution was ratified in 1791, the change became complete. The "takings clause" of that amendment stipulates that the government will give "just compensation" if private land is taken for public use. By making a law about how a government purchases land from its citizens, exclusive private property rights became official. The indigenous people, now more than ever, could be portrayed as outliers to civilization. They had no fences. They shared their resources. It was all suddenly unthinkable.

The United States, with a new relationship to land, created new arguments to justify grabbing every bit of soil on which the original occupants stood. In 1823, the case of Johnson v. M'Intosh came before the U.S. Supreme Court. Thomas Johnson had bought land from the Piankeshaw Tribe. William M'Intosh had supposedly received a land grant for some of the same land from the Federal Government, although it turns out that the two parcels did not actually overlap. But the facts were accepted as presented and the ruling stands. Chief Justice John Marshall, writing for a unanimous court, declared that, "While the different nations of Europe respected the rights of the natives as occupants, they asserted the ultimate dominion to be in themselves, and claimed and exercised, as a consequence of this ultimate dominion, a power to grant the soil while yet in the possession of the natives."[122]

The indigenous people were suddenly subsumed and consumed by a legal system that enshrined private property, especially if any white people wanted their land. They soon found themselves dispossessed with increasing frequency and violence. In 1864, to mention an especially egregious example, the U.S. Army descended on a Cheyenne and Arapaho village at Sand Creek, Colorado, killing and mutilating as many as 150, most of whom were women and children. The mistake the Cheyenne and Arapaho made was signing a treaty for land that turned out to have gold in it.

It seems like colonizers love gold. An 1868 treaty had given the seemingly worthless Black Hills to the natives in perpetuity. But in the mid-1870s, with the discovery of gold, perpetuity lost its meaning. As the Sioux holy man Black Elk said, white people "had found much of the yellow metal that they worship and that makes them crazy, and they wanted to have a road up through our country to where the yellow metal was."[123] The Sioux and Cheyenne refused to sell any land or lease mineral rights. They were deemed "hostile" by the government, and the army moved in to make the land safe for gold-miners.

In June 1876, General Custer and his cavalry attacked a native encampment, but neither Custer nor any of his soldiers survived the attack. For the natives, it was a successful act of self-defense. For the U.S. Government, it was an unconscionable massacre of their troops. Secretary of War William Tecumseh Sherman declared that the tribes had violated the treaty of 1868 by going to war with the United States. The Cheyenne and Sioux, having been invaded, were justifiably confused. But with the treaty supposedly broken, the army really poured in. Everyone was disarmed and forced onto reservations. Fugitive bands were hunted down, slaughtered, or arrested. Sitting Bull fled to Canada. Crazy Horse was caught and stabbed with a bayonet while in captivity and died. Then the U.S. Government carved the faces of some of its most powerful surveyors into a mountain.

More than a century later, dispossession and disregard continue apace, but now it's not just gold driving injustices against the indigenous, but fracked oil as well. And private property laws are one of the main tools used to make this happen. The Dakota Access Pipeline, designed to move crude oil from the Bakken Formation in western North Dakota, through both Dakotas, Iowa, and into Illinois where it might become less crude and more refined, *was* going to cross under the Missouri River north of the mostly white city of Bismarck. But the citizens complained that this could destroy their drinking water. The route was changed so that it passed under the river a half-mile north of the Standing Rock Reservation through land and under water that had been seized against the tribe's will in September 1958, through legislation passed by Congress that stated, "Any interest Indians may have in the bed of the Missouri River so far as it is within the boundaries of the Standing Rock Reservation, are hereby taken by the United States for the Oahe Project on the Missouri River."[124] When the Dakota Access Pipeline was rerouted through land that was "hereby taken," the people on the reservation, like the people of Bismarck, complained about threats to their water. But rather than another rerouting, they were met with pepper spray, rubber bullets, and attack dogs.

In September 2016, Judge James Boasberg ruled that the tribe had been sufficiently consulted and the pipeline could proceed. His statement claims that "A project of this magnitude often necessitates an extensive federal appraisal and permitting process. Not so here. Domestic oil pipelines, unlike natural-gas pipelines, require no general approval from the federal government. In fact, DAPL needs almost no federal permitting of *any* kind because 99% of its route traverses private land."[125] So if you own a piece of land, pretty much as long as you're not sacrificing children or making methamphetamines, you can do whatever you want and no one can stop you. James Boasberg is a judge. It's his job to interpret the law. He ruled that "the Tribe has not shown it will suffer injury that would be prevented by any injunction the Court could issue."[126] In a technical, lawyerly sense, he may be correct. Put a pipeline through private land, and no one can legally complain. But from the perspective of the Earth and its inhabitants' common interests, he is completely wrong—especially since the laws and precedents he is interpreting were made in the aftermath of atrocious and embarrassing cases like Johnson v. M'Intosh. As Kiana Heron writes, the "protests at Standing Rock today can only be fully understood in light of this colonial legacy, which from the beginning proclaimed that native lands were empty, and that native people, were, in effect, nothing more than the rocks, the trees, the water that they now so valiantly strive to protect."[127]

The very same day Judge Boasberg issued his ruling, a pipeline in Alabama broke and spilled 250,000 gallons of oil. The governor declared a state of emergency.[128] The very next day, a pipeline in Texas leaked about 33,000 gallons of oil.[129] And this is not just some strange coincidence. Angry gnomes were not trying to make this judge look foolish. Pipelines fail almost constantly. According to the United States' Pipelines and Hazardous Materials and Safety Administration, there have been more than 10,000 pipeline failures already this century. Pipelines are a terrible invention, even exempting the fracking that fills them or the fossil fuels they bring us to burn. They just break all the time. But if they're built on private property, no one can complain. Private property is sacrosanct. It's your land, do as you will.

But maybe instead of worrying about one person's supposed right to profit off private land, maybe we should worry about how we can all continue to live on our shared planet. To quote Tom Goldtooth of the Indigenous Environmental Network, "Our spiritual leaders are opposed to the privatization of our lands, which means the commoditization of the nature, water, air we hold sacred."[130]

I was at the Oceti Sakowin Camp in Standing Rock in November 2016, which is situated on the disputed land "hereby taken" in 1958, and meant to obstruct the completion of the Dakota Access Pipeline. The very same day The Army Corps of Engineers issued the camp an eviction notice, one of the water protectors pointed out to me the ways the government had closed roads and seized hills so that "They are leaving us with no option but to trespass."[131] Police and National Guard stood along arbitrary and debatable boundary lines. Behind those police, the pipeline was being laid. Anyone who crossed onto that land could be arrested for trespassing. No other crimes were required.

The sheer volume of law enforcement brought in to protect a pipeline by enforcing trespassing laws was outlandish. The night we arrived, it was too late and too dark to drive to the camp and set up a tent without being a nuisance to people trying to sleep off the sting of rubber bullets. We stopped in Bismarck, pulled into a hotel, and saw more than half the parking lot was filled with police vehicles. Scared, we went to another hotel. This one was better. Instead of more than half, slightly less than half the parking lot was cop cars. It seemed marginally safer. We stayed there. The next day, trying to get to Standing Rock, we encountered a roadblock, turned around, and took a different route. Trucks heading toward the camp were pulled over and searched. Military helicopters flew above. Trespassers beware.

An entire continent has been surveyed, sold, and turned into private property that can be ripped up and turned into rubble. If anyone objects, the police turn up to protect the right to make rubble. Our collective needs don't matter. The commons have become a piece of the past, receding from lived experience and into the history books. Need, intent, and collective interest have become irrelevant to land use. Who bought it? That's all anyone needs to know.

We're told this is normal. This is reality and we had better get used to it. But now is the aberration. The commons existed for millennia. Private property has existed for a few centuries. Our current system is the anomaly. We do not need to live this way.

So it is perhaps only now that someone could sell the stars and no one would think it's all that weird, when the Earth is no longer our common inheritance, but a conglomerate of commodities circling the sun. We divide it up and do as we will. And at night, we look into the sky and watch distant products twinkle. But why not? If we can buy and sell almost any piece of the Earth, why not buy the rest of the Universe?

Of course, what the International Star Registry does is pretty harmless, especially compared to buying land to put in a leaky pipeline. People don't destroy their stars after purchasing them. They just show their friends their parchment proofs of purchase and their maps of coordinates. But the very fact that the International Star Registry could be created and continue to exist says a great deal about how far we are from having a reasonable approach to living.

If we don't eradicate the mentality that makes the International Star Registry possible, if we continue to slice up our planet, and declare this chunk yours and that chunk mine, we'll just slice it up until there's nothing left but dust. We certainly don't need to return to feudal or tribal systems of land management. The future will be different from any past or present. But we don't need to accept what we have. A planet composed of private land, surrounded by stars for sale, is not one we have to tolerate. Exclusive private property is relatively new. We can make it history.

TIME IS NOT MONEY

Time is money. But time is a human construct. And so is money. But this does not mean these things are not real. Many human constructs are real. Buildings are real. Cars are real. Even hatred is real. Time and money are real. We just made them up.

So time is money. A simple enough sentence. An equivalence. Just like two and two is four, the items on either side of "is" are equal. Because each side is equivalent, we can and do sell our time for money. But the only transferable time is the highly artificial and contrived kind kept by our clocks and calendars. We do this because we need money—exchangeable units of value—to survive, pay our debts, and stay out of trouble with the authorities. Money is a social relation. The only reality it has is the reality we choose to give it.

Money arose as an intermediary between goods and as a means to tabulate debt. Rather than determining the relative value between every two bartered items, each is judged against a third. Initially, it was something like goats, cloth, stones, or whatever easily attained, non-monopolized commodity had become the mediator of exchange. But such items may be perishable or non-standard. They may fluctuate in value due to scarcity or production costs.

Precious metals can be minted in standard sizes and shapes and won't rot, and so they entered into common—but not universal—use. But even precious metals are a commodity among commodities, and this can cause confusion. In England in the late 1600s, raw silver and gold had a higher value than these same materials as minted money. Clever crooks began clipping coins, melting the clippings, selling these melted clippings for more coins, and then starting the whole process over again. Clipped and unclipped coins circulated together. Perhaps not surprisingly, the clipped coins were treated exactly the same as the untouched ones. A shilling was still a shilling, no matter what it weighed.

The philosopher John Locke entered the ensuing debate and declared that gold and silver possess a "natural" value that predates the state. According to Locke, it was time to pull the ruined coins and mint new ones that matched their "natural" value. But the rampant practice of recognizing any shilling as a shilling shows Locke's error. Money is carried for its purchasing power. If that power remains unchanged, the weight and shape of the money doesn't matter. Values are assessed and exchanges are made by social practice. Humans may ascribe value to bits and pieces of the natural world, but this is done without nature's consent. There are no "natural" values.

We now use fiat money—money disconnected from any commodity. But however value is assessed, all forms of money are arbitrary. It's not like people print money based on how much value there is "out there in the world. Value does not exist independent of social practice. We just print money. And then it exists, and has a value. We can choose or refuse to recognize it. Of course, we are compelled and coerced to recognize it.

And so we sell our time. But this time, like our money, is a purely social product. Time can be bisected, divided, and measured in any number of ways. It is gauged in relation to physical events. The tick of a clock. The swing of a pendulum. The vibration of an atom. The rotation of the Earth. Years, minutes, and seconds are not part of the Universe. We may create these units in relation to natural phenomena, but we are not required to do so. It's a lot like placing a political boundary along a river or a mountain range. In both cases, we apply an element of nature to a social practice, but there is really nothing natural about it.

Time is a confounding subject. Is it even real? Does it exist independent of our minds? As Saint Augustine writes in his *Confessions*, "What is time? Who can explain this easily and briefly? Who can comprehend this even in thought so as to articulate the answer in words? Yet what do we speak of, in our familiar everyday conversation, more than of time?

We surely know what we mean when we speak of it. We also know what we mean when we hear someone else talking about it. What then is time? Provided that no one asks me, I know. If I want to explain it to an inquirer, I do not know."[132]

Some have argued that time is unreal by portraying it as a series of points. The argument goes something like the following. Since the past is gone, lost to all but memory, and the future hasn't arrived yet, the present is the only time we have. And how long is that? An instant? And how long is an instant? A nanosecond? The blink of an eye? It turns out that the present conceived as a point cannot have a duration. If it did, we could then divide that duration into a past, present and future, and then that present could be further divided, on and on forever. So is that it? Is time unreal because the present is the only time we have and that is no time at all?

Much like Zeno's similar arguments against motion, such allegations of the unreality of time fail because they have no relation to our experience. Time, like motion, is perceived as a continuum. The ticking of a clock marks time because we remember the previous tick and anticipate the impending tock. There is a mental retention of the past that is linked to our experience of the present and an expected future. A series of perceptions does not yield temporal passage. Perceptions need to be unified into a sequence.

This temporal passage is constructed in our minds, after events occur. Separate neural pathways receive distinct signals—sights, sounds, smells, tastes, and tactile sensations— which then travel to the brain at various finite velocities. These signals arrive at different moments, leaving the brain the difficult task of reassembling all this information to try to figure out what just happened. We live in reality's wake. So is time purely mental? Does it exist in the Universe or only after our minds put it together?

Although it may remain beyond our grasp, there does seem to be a form of temporality we perceive but do not create. Rivers run to the sea, and stones turn to sand, but not because we will the future into the present. But what is this external temporality, and how do experience it? How do we perceive the Universe as it flows around and through us?

Before relativity, when Newtonian mechanics dominated our understanding of the physical world, space and time were treated as separate entities, both of which were universal, absolute, and independent of perspective. Time flowed equably. Space had verifiable positions. But Einstein showed that there is no difference between space and time. There is only spacetime, and there is nothing universal about it. Only *relationships* between aspects of the Universe are observable. If you found yourself floating through space, you would have no way to judge your velocity. You would first need to determine what you were moving in relation to. Is it that planet? That star over there? Or maybe that galaxy? Being based on matter in relative motion, time has no verifiability beyond a single frame of reference, and each of these questions will produce a different answer.

Einstein asks us to imagine one person riding on a train and another standing on the ground as the train passes. Two flashes of lightning occur. One is in front of the train. The other is behind it. The person on the ground perceives these flashes as simultaneous. The person on the train, moving toward one flash and away from the other, sees the flash the train is approaching first. Simultaneity is only ever apparent simultaneity. There is no way to know what really happened when.

In his *Confessions*, besides addressing just how baffling time is, Saint Augustine discusses the theological problem of just what God did in all that time before creation. After all, isn't the sudden decision to make a Universe a bit out of character for an eternally constant being? Augustine astutely points out, centuries before Einstein, that time requires matter. The question of what God did "then" misses the point since there was no "then" when there were no things. Time is dependent on matter in motion. There is not space and time. There is only spacetime. This is much more than a semantic distinction, as it impacts our understanding of what the Universe is and how we perceive it.

So there are not many things more artificial than the time kept by our clocks and calendars. Yet this socially constructed time is not only accepted, it has become one of the main tools we use to dominate and control one another. We are told that time is money, and we dutifully sell carefully measured pieces of our lives to the highest bidder in exchange for the means to stay alive. Time is money. And like the time kept by clocks and calendars, money is also a human creation, only even more obviously so.

In Joseph Conrad's *The Secret Agent*, a spy embedded in London's anarchist underworld is threatened with dismissal unless he fulfills his role as an *agent provocateur* and does some actual provoking. He is assigned the task of blowing up the Greenwich Observatory, the site of the prime meridian, the basis for the world's time zones, and a symbol of officially standardized time. Joseph Conrad was not sympathetic to anarchism, and the *Secret Agent* is filled with irony and satire. But despite that satire, an element of satori still shines through. The time kept by our clocks and the money kept by our banks are a product of socially constructed spacetime. This spacetime is much more than a medium of movement. Its logic and structure determine the limits of the possible. Changing the world will involve changing the ways we navigate spacetime. Clocks are a worthy target.

Because we have made time and money equivalent, money permeates all our time, as well as our space. It is spacetime, after all. Before the capitalist era, wealth was created and maintained mainly through land ownership. Money and merchants were relegated to the ports and periphery. The wealthy were the landed aristocracy, and they did not sully their good names by engaging in trade. The transition from wealth through land ownership to wealth through the investment in marketable goods brought commerce from the periphery and into everyday life. As time spent producing these goods became increasingly important, clock towers replaced cathedrals. The overland trade routes traversed mostly by merchants became less unique, as every stretch of road became a trade route and every citizen a merchant.

The logic of commerce produced and produces our spacetime. Our bodies extend into it, and we become tied to its rhythms. Through this interaction, we create an identity. We value, prize, and defend it. But it is produced by a constellation of historically situated forces. A constructed self in a constructed reality. From birth, we are educated and molded to "properly" navigate produced spacetime. We are conditioned and encased. We are like machines, designed and capable of amazing tasks, but only within the limits of that design. Without a rebellion from the given, there can be no true creativity. One of our most debilitating notions is the belief that what exists must exist. We can and should disconnect from the given. This will entail the total rejection of habit, a complete mental revolt, and the refusal of all ideological conditioning.

Now everybody—

WALKING EACH OTHER HOME

We're all just walking each other home.

RAM DASS

He was young and he was lost. But the nameless narrator in Alejandro Zambra's *Ways of Going Home* found his house all by himself. His parents looked all over for him. But when they got home, he was already there.

"You went a different way," my mother said later, angry, her eyes still swollen.

You were the one who went a different way, I thought,
but I didn't say it.[133]

There are many ways of going home.

In "This Must Be the Place" by the Talking Heads, David
Byrne sings, "Home is where I want to be, but I guess I'm
already there."[134] He has described this song as a "series
of non sequiturs, phrases that may have strong emotional
resonance but don't have any narrative qualities."[135] Yet even
adrift in this sea of non-narrative non sequiturs, the word
"home" still retains its powers. Just speaking or singing the
word can act as a potent, even magical, incantation.

"Home. Everybody wants to go home. Even when they're
old. Even when they're small."[136] These constitute all the
lyrics to the song "Home" by the band Low. It may seem
brief, but there's really no need to elaborate. We all know
what it means. After all, everybody wants to go home.

I spent the first part of my childhood living in a house at
the end of a gravel road. Our backyard led directly into a
large cluster of trees containing dirt paths and secret forts.
Beyond those trees, a field filled with wild strawberries led

to another group of trees and an old, rusting truck. These are the places the word "home" conjures for me. Not just the house, but the land around it, the places where the area children would gather, play, and explore.

Once, I knocked on my neighbor's door to see if he wanted to come outside, but he told me he would rather watch *Star Trek*. I slammed the door on his head. His parents were very upset. My parents grounded me. But I think I had a point.

◈

They still air *Star Trek* reruns, but the woods are gone. The gravel road is paved. It no longer dead ends, but extends into the new subdivision that has supplanted the woods, the field, and the abandoned truck. Enclosed spaces with lockable doors have replaced the open spaces I still think of as my first home.

◈

A home is not simply four walls or a fixed residence. It is a widely variable set of circumstances in which self, society, and nature can sit in a dynamic, collaborative relationship. The materials of home flow in and out, forever in flux, creating a place where our ever-shifting selves can develop and thrive. We have a physical home, a cultural home, a geographic home. We may be at home in the countryside, at home in the city, or we may not even feel at home in our own skin. But a home is where we can be or become ourselves. It doesn't matter if we've ever even been there. Just imagining its outline is enough to inspire longing.

❖

The place I think of as my first home no longer exists in any meaningful sense. All my favorite parts have been bulldozed. I cannot return.

But it was only ever an abstraction in a child's mind. Now it's an adult's memory of a child's abstraction. Of course I cannot return. Just where would I go? A home is only ever an idea. It is imaginary. But it is real.

❖

As Ursula K. Le Guin writes,

> Home, imagined, comes to be. It is real, realer than any other place, but you can't get to it unless your people show you how to imagine it—whoever your people are. They may not be your relatives. They may never have spoken your language. They may have been dead for a thousand years. They may be nothing but words printed on paper, ghosts of voices, shadows of minds. But they can guide you home.[137]

❖

If external conditions make a home unimaginable,
it can't exist.

When you have no ground on which to stand, your
imagination can't take you very far.

❖

Humans arose in what is now called Ethiopia. Since then,
seeking home, we have covered the globe.

❖

If we say we are sending refugees escaping famines or wars
back to their "homes," it is a misuse of the word. They can
hopefully find a home, but it probably won't be found at
their place of origin.

And when teenagers leave abusive families, they may be
running away, but they are not running away from home. A
home is their goal, not their point of departure.

This is why "homeless" describes the state of "homelessness"
so well. Renaming the homeless "street people" or something
misses the point. The street is not the problem. Homelessness—
the lack of a multifaceted, sustaining environment—is. And
many more of us are homeless than we might like to imagine.

❖

In *The Wizard of Oz*, both the novel from 1900 and the film from 1938, a tornado blows Dorothy Gale from Kansas to the Land of Oz. She seeks the aid of a wizard to help her return, but the wizard accidently flies away without her. She appears to be stranded forever. In the film version, Glinda the Good Witch of the North finally informs Dorothy that "You've always had the power to go home."[138] The magic slippers she has been wearing can take her there. Dorothy's face is then lit unlike any other moment in the movie. Through the power of film, we see that she is enlightened. She has always had the power to get home, but external forces were making this simple task seem impossible.

❖

Dorothy Gale was uprooted by a natural disaster. Another Dorothy, Dorothy Day, was eight years old and living in Oakland when the great earthquake of 1906 struck. As she later wrote of the earthquake's aftermath:

> What I remember most plainly about the earthquake was the human warmth and kindness of everyone afterward. For days refugees poured out of burning San Francisco and camped in Idora Park and the race track in Oakland. … Mother and all our neighbors were busy from morning to night cooking hot meals. They gave away every extra garment they possessed. They stripped themselves to the bone in giving, forgetful of the morrow. While the crisis lasted, people loved each other.[139]

Disasters can quite literally tear down the walls around us, take away our isolated atomism, and necessitate new ways of interacting. When the existing order crumbles, new systems can arise spontaneously, ones often based on care and compassion. We can learn to love each other. A home made invisible and impossible by our collective isolation suddenly becomes visible and inhabitable.

❖

Every being, every bit of matter, is at the center of its universe. An endless plurality of centers overlap and interact. We travel like turtles, our homes on our backs, pulling a universe along with us.

When I enter your home, I bring mine in with me.

Treat everyone like an invited guest. Behave like an invited guest. Help others meet their needs. Provide them with comfort. Enter others' spaces politely and respectfully. Remove your shoes if asked. Help with the dishes. Play with the children.

Wherever you are, remember, you are in someone's home.

❖

A few years after the nameless narrator in *Ways of Going Home* found his own way home, there was an earthquake. "The night of the earthquake was the first time that I realized everything could come tumbling down. Now I think it's a good thing to know. It's necessary to remember it every second."[140]

The existing institutions that keep so many of us incapable of creating a home could crumble at any moment. When they crumble, we could live in better, more benevolent ways. We could learn to love each other. We could learn to live as neighbors. But do we really need to wait for total collapse? Or can we just make sure everyone gets home safely? Can we start living in ways that make sense? Can we find our own way home?

Everyone, please, make yourselves at home.

NOTES

1   Naomi Klein, "Can Climate Change Unite the Left?" *In These Times*, October 13, 2014.

2   Talking Heads, "(Nothing But) Flowers," *Naked*. Warner Bros., LP. Released March 1988.

3   Mark 13:24-25 (King James).

4   Mark 13:30.

5   Heb. 1:1-2.

6   1 John 2:18.

7   Charles Mackay, *Extraordinary Popular Delusions and the Madness of Crowds* (1841: New York: Three Rivers Press, 1980), 269-70.

8   See https://en.wikipedia.org/wiki/Sheldan_Nidle.

9   Noam Chomsky, "The End of History?" *In These Times*,
        September 4, 2014.

10   "Werner Herzog: Trust in My Wild Fantasies," *The Talks*,
        January 30, 2013.

11   Bill McKibben, "Global Warming's Terrifying New Math,"
        Rolling Stone, July 19, 2012.

12   Francis. *Laudato Si: Praise Be To You; On Care for Our Common
        Home* (Vatican City, Italy: Libreria Editrice Vatanica, 2015), [161].

13   Mike Watt, "Shore Duty," *Contemplating the Engine Room*.
        Columbia, LP. Released 1997.

14   John H. Richardson, "When the End of Human Civilization is
        Your Day Job," *Esquire*, July 7, 2015.

15   Ibid.

16   Ibid.

17   "Werner Herzog: Trust In My Wild Fantasies."

18   Miguel de Unamuno, *Our Lord Don Quixote*, (1905: Princeton:
        Princeton University Press, 1967), 16.

19   Klein, "Can Climate Change Unite the Left?"

20   Bill Callahan, "One Fine Morning," *Apocalypse*. Drag City, LP.
        Released 2011.

21   Alan Moore, *Promethea: Collected Edition*; Book 5, (New York:
        DC Comics, 2003).

22   Francis, *Laudato Si*, [95].

23   Sun Ra, *It's After the End of the World*. BASF, LP. Released 1972.

24   Samuel Beckett, *Endgame: A Play in One Act* (New York: Grove
        Press, 1958), 11.

25   Ibid., 13.

26   Ibid., 78.

27   Revelation 20: 1-2, 4.

28 Richard Francis, *Ann the Word: The Story of Ann Lee, Female Messiah, Mother of the Shakers, The Woman Clothed with the Sun* (New York: Arcade Publishing, 2013), 25.

29 Ibid., 71.

30 Deborah E. Burns, *Shaker Cities of Peace, Love, and Union: A History of the Hancock Bishopric* (Hanover, NH: University Press of New England, 1993), 14.

31 Francis, *Ann the Word*, 336.

32 "'What Must I Do?' at the End of the World," *Woodbine*, May 16, 2014.

33 Mohandas Gandhi, *The Bhagavad Gita According to Gandhi* (1930: Berkeley: Berkeley Hills Books, 2000), 37.

34 *The Richmond Whig*, November 10, 1859.

35 Henry David Thoreau, "A Plea For Captain John Brown," October 1859.

36 Martin Luther King, Jr. *The Autobiography of Martin Luther King, Jr.* (New York: Grand Central Publishing, 2001), 14.

37 Mohandas Gandhi, "For Passive Resisters," *Indian Opinion*, October 26, 1907.

38 Henry David Thoreau, "On Civil Disobedience," 1849.

39 Thoreau, "A Plea For Captain Brown."

40 Mohandas Gandhi, "The Jews," *Harijan*, November 26, 1938.

41 Ibid.

42 Saul Alinsky, *Rules for Radicals: A Pragmatic Primer for Realistic Radicals* (1971: New York, Vantage, 1989), 41.

43 Isaac Deutscher, *The Prophet Armed: Trotsky 1879-1921* (1954: New York: Verso, 2003), 349.

44 Ibid., 417.

45 Ibid., 428.

46 Rebecca Solnit, "Call climate change what it is: violence," *The*

Guardian, April 7, 2014.

47   Natasha Lennard and Adrian Parr, "Our Crime Against the Planet, and Ourselves," *The New York Times*, May 18, 2016.

48   Chaitanya Mallapur, "61% Rise In Heat-Stroke Deaths Over Decade," *India Spend*, May 27, 2015.

49   Nida Najar and Hari Kumar, "Pray for Shade: Heat Wave Sets a Record in India," *The New York Times*, May 20, 2016.

50   Ian Johnston, "Farmer Suicides Soar in India as Deadly Heatwave Hits 51 Degrees Celsius," *The Independent*, May 20, 2016.

51   John Vidal, "Across Africa, The Worst Food Crisis Since 1985 looms for 50 Million," *The Guardian*, May 22, 2016.

52   Mark Petersen et al, "2016 One-Year Seismic Hazard Forecast for the Central and Eastern United States from Induced and Natural Earthquakes," (2016: U.S. Geologic Survey), 14.

53   http://www.legis.state.tx.us/BillLookup/Text.aspx?LegSess=84R&Bill=HB40

54   Ibid.

55   Michael Wines, "Colorado Court Strikes Down Local Bans on Fracking," *The New York Times*, May 2, 2016.

56   "City of Fort Collins vs. Colorado Oil and Gas Association," http://www.courts.state.co.us. May 2, 2016.

57   Elisabeth Malkin and Alberto Arce, "Berta Cáceres, Indigenous Activist, Is Killed in Honduras," *The New York Times*, March 3, 2016.

58   Hillary Clinton, *Hard Choices* (New York: Simon & Schuster, 2014), 266.

59   Ambassador Hugo Llorens, "TFHO1: OPEN AND SHUT: THE CASE OF THE HONDURAN COUP," July 24, 2009, *Wikileaks*.

60   "Hear Hillary Clinton Defend Her Role in Honduras Coup When Questioned by Juan González," *Democracy Now*, April 13, 2016.

61   Thoreau, "On Civil Disobedience."

62   Derrick Jensen, *Endgame: Volume I: The Problem of Civilization* (New York: Seven Stories Press, 2006), 81.

63   David Graeber, *Direct Action: An Anthology* (Oakland: AK Press, 2009), 456-7.

64   Natasha Lennard and Nicholas Mirzoeff, "What Protest Looks Like," *The New York Times*, August 3, 2016.

65   *If A Tree Falls: A Story of the Earth Liberation Front*, directed by Marshall Curry (2011, Oscilloscope), DVD.

66   Klein, "Can Climate Change Unite the Left?"

67   Dave Foreman, "Earth First!," *Earth First!*, February 1982.

68   Dave Foreman et al, eds., *Earth First*, November 1980.

69   "4 Accused of Sabotage Plot," *The New York Times*, June 1, 1989.

70   Oliver Gillham, *The Limitless City: A Primer on the Urban Sprawl Debate* (Washington, DC: Island Press, 2002), xv.

71   *If A Tree Falls*, Marshall Curry.

72   Dalai Lama, Twitter Post, April 1, 2016, 2:30 a.m., https://twitter.com/DalaiLama.

73   "Militant Feminism: An Explosive Interview With a KKKanadian Urban Guerrilla," *Earth First!*, March 2010.

74   Ann Hansen, *Direct Action: Memoirs of an Urban Guerrilla* (Oakland: AK Press, 2002), 273.

75   Ibid., 147.

76   http://www.prisontv.net/blog-about-prison-issues-crime-and-punishment/8/2011-Feb-05/squamish-5-and-the-litton-bombing

77   See, http://primitivism.com/kaczynski.htm

78   Theodore Kaczynski, "Industrial Society and Its Future," 1995, paragraph 5.

79   *If A Tree Falls*, Marshall Curry.

80   *Earth First!*, May 1999.

81   Stanley Milgram, *Obedience to Authority: An Experimental View* (New York: Harper & Row, 1974), 4.

82   Cage quoted in Kay Larson, *Where the Heart Beats: John Cage, Zen Buddhism, and the Inner Life of Artists* (New York: The Penguin Press, 2012).

83   Andrew Rathman, Danielle Allen and Frank Bidart, "An Interview with Frank Bidart,"*Chicago Review* 47, no. 3 (2001), 26.

84   William Shakespeare, *King Lear*. (1608: Oxford: Oxford University Press, 2001), 131-32.

85   Garry Wills, *Lincoln at Gettysburg* (New York: Touchstone, 1992), 38.

86   Ibid.

87   Walt Whitman, *Democratic Vistas* (1871: Amsterdam: Fredonia Books, 2002), 40.

88   This is Emma Goldman's most famous remark, despite the fact that it seems she never said (or wrote) it. This popular misquotation is rumored to have derived from an attempt to fit the following passage from *Living My Life* on a t-shirt:

"At the dances I was one of the most untiring and gayest. One evening a cousin of Sasha, a young boy, took me aside. With a grave face, as if he were about to announce the death of a dear comrade, he whispered to me that it did not behoove an agitator to dance. Certainly not with such reckless abandon, anyway. It was undignified for one who was on the way to become a force in the anarchist movement. My frivolity would only hurt the Cause.

I grew furious at the impudent interference of the boy. I told him to mind his own business, I was tired of having the Cause constantly thrown into my face. I did not believe that a cause which stood for a beautiful ideal, for anarchism, for release and freedom from conventions and prejudice, should demand the denial of life and joy. I insisted that our Cause could not expect me to become a nun and that the movement should not be turned into a cloister. If it meant that, I did not want it. I want freedom, the right to self-expression, everybody's right to beautiful, radiant things."

See Emma Goldman, *Living My Life* vol. 1 (1931: New York: Dover, 1970), 56. In its full glory, rather than pithy paraphrase, this passage manages to depict the sober seriousness of most "revolutionaries." But it's nice the other way too, and fits much better on a t-shirt.

89   Vaclav Havel, *Disturbing the Peace: A Conversation with Karel Hvížďala* (New York: Vintage Books, 1990), 113.

90   Garry Trudeau, "The Abuse of Satire," *The Atlantic*, April 11, 2015.

91   See Arthur Koestler, *The Act of Creation* (New York: Macmillan, 1964). The terms are his, not mine.

92   Ibid., 21.

93   Ibid., 35-36.

94   Mikhail Bakhtin, *The Dialogic Imagination* (Austin, TX: University of Texas Press, 1981), 304-5.

95   Marc Maron and Chris Rock, "WTF Podcast," Episode 224, November 3, 2011 (Available at www.wtfpod.com)

96   Ibid., 176.

97   Ibid., 154.

98   Marc Maron and Conan O'Brien, "WTF Podcast," Episode 163, April 4, 2011 (Available at www.wtfpod.com)

99   Christopher Hitchens, *Arguably* (Twelve: New York, 2011), 392.

100   R.C. Harvey, "At Swords' Point: Humor as Weapon," The Comics Journal, December 19, 2011.

101   Richard Rorty, *Truth and Progress* (Cambridge: Cambridge

University Press, 1998), 203.

102 Swords quoted in Harvey, "At Swords' Point," Betty Swords' *Humor Power* remains an unpublished manuscript.

103 Simone de Beauvoir, *The Second Sex* (1949: New York: Vintage Books, 2011), 156.

104 Ibid., 45-46.

105 David Foster Wallace, *Consider the Lobster and Other Essays* (New York: Back Bay Books, 2006), 104.

106 Bakhtin, *Dialogic Imagination*, 295

107 Thomas Merton, "Gandhi and the One-Eyed Giant," in *Gandhi on Non-Violence*, edited by Thomas Merton (New York: New Directions, 1964), 3.

108 Karl Mathiesen, "Embrace of the Serpent star: 'My tribe is nearly extinct,'" *The Guardian*, June 8, 2016.

109 David Berman, *Actual Air* (New York: Open City Books, 1999), 58.

110 Alice M. Isen, "Positive Affect Facilitates Creative Problem Solving," *Journal of Personality and Social Psychology* 52, no. 6 (1987), 1123.

111 Ibid., 1128.

112 And there aren't many things funnier than bodily fluids.

113 Allegra Kirkland, "White Nationalist PAC Blankets Iowa With Robocalls For Trump," *Talking Points Memo*, January 9, 2016.

114 Murray Bookchin, *The Ecology of Freedom, The Emergence and Dissolution of Hierarchy* (Palo Alto, CA: Cheshire Books, 1982), 366.

115 Whitman, *Democratic Vistas*, 1, emphasis added.

116 Swords quoted in Harvey, "At Swords' Point."

117 See www.iau.org/public/themes/buying_star_names/

118 See www.starregistry.com

119 David Herbert Donald, *Lincoln* (New York: Simon & Schuster, 1995), 52.

120 Theodore Roosevelt quoted in Kathleen Dalton, *Theodore Roosevelt: A Strenuous Life* (New York: Knopf, 2002), 126.

121 John R. Stilgoe, *Common Landscapes of America, 1580 to 1845* (New Haven: Yale University Press, 1982), 48.

122 Johnson & Grahm's Lessee v. M'Intosh, 21 U.S. (8 Wheat.) 543, 574 (1823).

123 Black Elk, *Black Elk Speaks: Being the Life of a Holy Man of the Oglala Sioux* (1932: Lincoln: University of Nebraska Press, 1961), 9.

124 Public Law 85-915, September 2, 1958.

125 Standing Rock Sioux Tribe v. U.S. Army Corps of Engineers, United States District Court for the District of Coulmbia. Civil Action No. 16-1534 (JEB), 2.

126 Ibid., 1-2.

127 Kiana Herold, "Terra Nullius and the History of Broken Treaties at Standing Rock," *Intercontinental Cry*, November 14, 2016.

128 "State of emergency declared after crucial oil pipeline leaks 250,000 gallons in Alabama," *KFOR*, September 16, 2016.

129 "U.S. regulator orders inquiry, repairs after Sunoco's Permian leak," *Reuters*, September 15, 2016.

130 "Trump advisors aim to privatize oil-rich Indian reservations," *Reuters*, December 5, 2016.

131 Personal conversation, recorded November 25, 2016.

132 Saint Augustine, *Confessions* (400: Oxford: Oxford World's Classics, 2008), 230.

133 Alejandro Zambra, *Ways of Going Home* (New York: Farrar, Straus and Giroux, 2011), 3.

134 Talking Heads, "This Must Be the Place," *Speaking In Tongues*.

Sire, LP. Released June 1, 1983.

135   David Gans, *Talking Heads: The Band & Their Music* (New York: Avon Books, 1985), 113.

136   Low, "Home," *Secret Name*. Kranky, LP. Released November 1998.

137   Ursula K. Le Guin, *Words Are My Matter: Writings About Life and Books 2000-2016* (Easthampton, MA: Small Beer Press, 2016), 5.

138   *The Wizard of Oz* (1939), directed by Victor Fleming (MGM 2013).

139   Dorothy Day, *From Union Square to Rome* (1938: Maryknoll, NY: Orbis Books, 2006), 24.

140   Zambra, *Ways of Going Home*, 137.

Lightning Source UK Ltd.
Milton Keynes UK
UKHW020623020222
398080UK00005B/182